Awesome Coconut Milk Recipes

Date: 3/4/15

641.6461 AWE
Awesome coconut milk
recipes : tasty ways to bring

Awesome Coconut Milk Recipes

Tasty Ways to Bring Coconuts from the Palm Tree to Your Plate

Edited and Introduced by Nicole Smith

Skyhorse Publishing

Skyhorse Publishing books may be purchased in bulk at special discounts for sales promotion, corporate gifts, fund-raising, or educational purposes. Special editions can also be created to specifications. For details, contact the Special Sales Department, Skyhorse Publishing, 307 West 36th Street, 11th Floor, New York, NY 10018 or info@skyhorsepublishing.com.

Skyhorse® and Skyhorse Publishing® are registered trademarks of Skyhorse Publishing, Inc.®, a Delaware corporation.

www.skyhorsepublishing.com

10 9 8 7 6 5 4 3 2 1

Library of Congress Cataloging-in-Publication Data is available on file.

Printed in China

ISBN: 978-1-62914-755-0

TABLE OF CONTENTS

SOUPS

MAIN COURSE

DESSERTS

DRINKS

Introduction

Calling all coconut lovers! You already know that coconut milk is amazing, and in this book we've captured the very best recipes that use this delicious drink! You'll find recipes spanning your whole meal starting with a tasty bowl of Spicy Tomato Coconut Soup and ending with delicious desserts like Chocolate Coconut Almond Ice Cream!

Coconut milk is not only tasty, but a great substitute for dairy. Each of these amazing recipes have been concocted by members of the Instructables community. With these recipes, there's sure to be something to suit everyone! You'll find Coconut Curry Lamb, Hawaiian Banana French Toast, and Sweet Potato Pie!

Follow these step-by-step directions with great photos to make your next meal amazing. Whether it's fresh milk from a coconut or opening a can, you're sure to find the best combination of recipes to create the perfect coconut milk inspired meal!

Nicole Smith
Instructables.com

wesome Coconut Milk Recipes

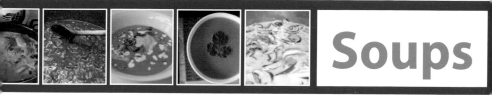

Soups

Tom Kha Gai Thai Coconut Soup

Spicy Tomato Coconut Soup

Vegan Coconut Curry Vegetable Soup

Peanut Butter Soup with Fufu

Spicy Semolina Porridge with Chicken and Vegetables

Thai Butternut Squash Soup with Chicken and Vegetables

Tasty Dahl Soup

Carrot Soup

White Gazpacho

Tom Kha Gai Thai Coconut Soup

by canida
www.instructables.com/id/
Tom-Kha-Gai-
Thai-Coconut-Soup/

Tom Kha Gai—Thai Coconut Soup. A traditional and tasty Thai soup, tthis is my favorite Thai restaurant staple, and an excellent twist on chicken soup for cold winter days. I'm a huge fan of coconut, chicken soup, and creamy soups in general, so it's a winner for me.

Of course, making it at home means I can customize it to my preferences. It's surprisingly easy to make! This recipe is loosely adapted from David Johnson's Thai Food, a brick-sized comprehensive guide to Thai cooking.

Note that you can make a pescatarian version (fish stock, shrimp instead of chicken) or even vegetarian or vegan (veggie stock, tofu for chicken, soy sauce for fish sauce) though the latter will lack some of the pungency that only comes with fish sauce.

Step 1: Tools and Ingredients

This recipe scales beautifully—just multiply the ingredients below. I've included substitutions for ingredients you may not have easily at hand, but a trip to an Asian grocery will handily turn up everything on this list. I buy lots of lemongrass and galanga ahead, then chop and freeze them in pre-sorted Ziploc bags for future use. They keep quite well. You can also do this with the shallots, coriander root, and kaffir lime leaves.

Broth:
- 1 can coconut milk
- 2–3 cups chicken stock (homemade is best, then the stuff in cartons; bouillon cubes are a last resort.)
- pinch of salt
- 1 teaspoon palm sugar (I usually substitute brown sugar)
- 2 stalks fresh lemongrass, washed and chopped in chunks (dried lemongrass is far inferior—punch it up with extra lime juice and zest at the end if you're forced to go this route)
- 3 red shallots, peeled and chunked (I often substitute 3 smashed cloves of garlic plus a bit of onion)
- 2 coriander roots, scraped (I usually substitute a pinch of whole coriander seed plus a handful of fresh coriander [cilantro] leaves)
- 2 chili peppers, halved (pick your favorite type, and modify number to suit your spice taste)

tom kha gai thai coconut soup

- 1.5" chunk of galanga root, chunked (ginger is in the same family but tastes totally different—galanga TOTALLY makes the flavor of this dish. If you can't get this locally, travel to a nearby city and visit the Asian markets or scour the internet, buy a pound, then freeze what you can't use now. It's a floral flavor that you'll definitely recognize if you've had tom kha gai before.)
- 3 kaffir lime leaves, coarsely chopped (I have a kaffir lime tree in my yard, but you can substitute lime zest if necessary. It just won't be as fragrant and complex.)
- 1 teaspoon chili garlic sauce (optional, and kind of a cheat, but often good.)

Chunks:
- 1 pound boneless skinless chicken thighs, cut to 1" pieces (you can use breasts, but the thighs are moister and tastier)
- 1 cup chopped mushrooms (your choice—mix it up)
- 1–3 tablespoons fish sauce (This stuff is pungent—if you're not familiar, add incrementally and taste before increasing. But don't be turned off by the smell. Definitely use some, as it's a key flavor that softens when you add it to the soup.)
- 1 can baby corn, drained and chopped to ½" chunks (optional)

Finish:
- 1 tablespoon lime juice (more if compensating—see notes above)
- 1 handful fresh cilantro, chopped
- ½ cup grape tomatoes halved or 2 plum tomatoes coarsely chopped (optional)

Tools:
- 1 large pot, at least 3 qt
- knife
- cutting board

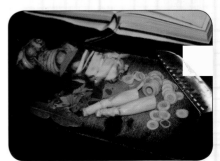

Step 3: Strain Broth

Pour through a sieve/strainer to remove chunks, and return the broth to your big pot. You can rescue a few items from the strainer, mince them, and return them to the pot if you like—I usually don't bother. You can usually smoosh more tasty liquid out of the chunks if you try, so give them a stiff squeeze.

Step 2: Make Broth

Combine all broth ingredients (coconut milk, stock, salt, sugar, shallots/garlic, coriander, galanga, lemongrass, kaffir lime leaves, chili sauce), bring to a low boil, and simmer for at least 15 minutes.

if using. Simmer lightly until chicken is cooked.

Step 5: Finish and Serve

Add the cilantro, tomatoes, and lime juice.

Taste—the soup should be fragrant, with a rich (read: nicely fatty) taste, and a mix of sweet/sour/salty flavors in the broth. You can tweak the latter with more sugar

Step 4: Add Chunks

Chop chicken, mushrooms, and baby corn and add to pot with broth. Add fish sauce and lime zest (sweet), lime juice (sour), or fish sauce (salty and tangy). Serve hot.

This soup keeps beautifully and will taste even better the next day after the flavors mingle overnight. You may want to hit it with a bit more fresh lime after reheating, though, just to keep it zippy.

This was my warming supper tonight. The weather has turned a lot colder the last few weeks and I've started craving the comforting warmth of bowls of homemade soup with thick slices of bread and butter. I made this soup with ingredients I had in my cupboard as I haven't had chance to get to the shops for a few days. For a store cupboard recipe, I have to say, this is pretty classy and well worth making.

Step 1: Ingredients

- 2 (400g) tins of tomatoes
- 2 tablespoons vegetable oil
- 1 medium onion, finely diced
- 2 teaspoons red chili flakes (adjust according to how spicy you want it)
- 2 teaspoons panch phoran (a Bengali 5 spice mix, available in larger supermarkets)
- 3 cm chunk of fresh ginger, peeled and grated
- 2 cloves of garlic, grated or crushed
- 2 teaspoon garam masala
- 400ml can of half fat coconut milk

Step 2:

Place a large saucepan over medium high heat, add the oil, and heat for a few seconds.

Step 3:

Add the onion to the pan and cook until translucent and soft.

Step 4:

Add the chili flakes and allow the spices to sizzle for around 30 seconds. Next add the panch phoran, ginger, and garlic and cook out for a minute or so.

Step 5:

Add the tinned tomatoes and simmer the mixture over medium heat for 10–15 minutes.

Step 6:

Stir through the garam masala and continue to cook for another 5–10 minutes until the tomatoes have thickened and taken on a rich, more orange color.

Step 7:

Add a generous pinch of salt and a teaspoon of sugar. Then either using a stick blender or food processor, blitz the soup until you have removed the lumps. This stage is optional but I prefer a smooth tomato soup.

Step 8:

Return the blended tomatoes to the saucepan, add the coconut milk, stir thoroughly and heat through for a few minutes.

Serve with either rice or a thick chunk of bread. I ate mine with my homemade pumpkin bread.

This delicious chunky vegetable curry soup is a great way to use up your vegetables at the end of the week. It's cheap to make, suitable for vegans and vegetarians and can feed up to four people.

Step 1: Ingredients

- half a cauliflower
- 1 large zucchini
- 1 large carrot
- ½ cup of chopped shallots
- 1 (400 ml) can of light coconut milk
- 1 tablespoon of vegetable stock powder, dissolved in 400ml of water
- 1 teaspoon of curry powder
- half a packet of rice noodles (optional)
- bean sprouts (to garnish)

Step 2:

Put a large saucepan on the stove and heat on high.

Chop zucchini, cauliflower, and carrot into bite-sized pieces (as shown) and add to the saucepan when hot.

Step 3:

Add the coconut milk to the saucepan. Fill up the empty can with hot water and dissolve one tablespoon of vegetable stock powder. Add the stock to the saucepan.

Step 4:

Add the curry powder to the saucepan and stir to dissolve.

Step 5:

Add chopped shallots to the saucepan and bring the soup to the boil.

Step 6:

If you wish, you can add some rice noodles to this soup.

Add the rice noodles to the soup while it is boiling. Turn the heat down to medium, place the lid on the saucepan, and simmer for around 8 minutes or until the noodles are soft.

Step 7:

Once the noodles are soft, turn off the heat and let the soup cool for a couple of minutes.

Step 8:

Ladle into bowls and top with some bean sprouts for some added crunch.

Enjoy!

Peanut Butter Soup and Fufu

by Jetty
www.instructables.com/id/
Peanut-Butter-
Soup-Fufu/

Peanut Butter Soup and Fufu. This is the best peanut soup you'll ever taste. It takes about an hour to make. Don't eat your spoon!

Step 1: Ingredients

- 1½ cups of peanut butter.
- chicken stock
- 1 pound of salty pork meat
- 1 onion
- 1 hot pepper
- celeriac
- 2 bay leaves
- 6 piment corn
- 2 tomatoes
- 2 pounds of chicken filet
- 1½ liters
  of water
- salt
- pepper

- 1 can of coconut milk
- 1 pack of fufu plantain
  Note: The peanut butter in the image is from Surinam. It is fiery hot. You can just as well use you own kind. It's good both spicy and not spicy.

Step 2: De-salt, Stock, Brown and Chop

Desalt your salty meat by cooking it for 5 minutes.

Make chicken stock (use a cube if you're not into this) and add the bay leaves, the piment, and the celeriac

Chop your onions and tomatoes very fine.

Step 4: Water Down the Peanut Butter

Put the peanut butter in a big pan and add the chicken stock until it gets watery.

Add the salty meat, the browned chicken filets, the tomatoes and the onion.

Add stock cubes or Aromat according to taste.

If you like spicy soup, add the chili.

Step 3: Brown the Filets

Cut your chicken filets into little pieces, add salt and pepper, and brown them in a hot frying pan.

Take the bay leaves out of the chicken stock.

Step 5: Cut and Cook

Cut your celeriac into fine pieces.

Cook your coconut milk until it starts foaming and reduce it a little.

Make the fufu.

Step 6: Make Your Fufu

Bring a cup of water to the boil in a saucepan.

Divide the water in 2 equal parts.

Add 110 grams of fufu flour to the pan and stir it with a wooden spoon until the water is absorbed by the fufu.

Gradually add the rest of the water.

Place over medium heat and heat thoroughly (I mean really thoroughly!) for about 4 minutes until a smooth but thick consistency is achieved.

Allow fufu to cool.

Step 7: Plating Up.

Put a little ball of fufu in the soup plate and pour the soup around.

Sprinkle with celeriac.

To finish drizzle a little coconut cream on top.

Enjoy!

Spicy Semolina Porridge with Chicken and Vegetables

by Ilma Nizam
www.instructables.com/id/
Spicy-Semolina-Porridge-
with-Chicken-
and-Vegetable/

Step 1: Ingredients

- semolina: 150 g
- chicken: 100 g
- chicken stock or water: 4 cups
- coconut milk: 3 cups
- carrots: 25 g
- leeks: 25 g
- cabbage: 25 g
- 1 tomato
- 1 teaspoon cumin powder
    salt and pepper to taste

For Temper:

- oil or ghee
- onion
- ginger
- garlic
- rampe
- curry leaves

Step 2: Method

Boil chicken—adding salt, pepper, and turmeric powder. Using your fingers, tear off pieces of chicken. Cut the vegetables into small pieces.

Heat the pot and add 4 cups of chicken stock or water. Then add the vegetables, chicken, salt, pepper, and cumin powder and leave it to cook for 5 minutes. Add semolina and coconut milk. Keep stirring for 3 to 5 minutes. Remove from heat.

Step 3: Tempering

Add ginger, garlic, onion, rampe, and curry leaves to oil or ghee.

Heat until it's golden brown and then pour it onto the semolina porridge and mix.

Voila! Your Spicy Semolina Porridge with Chicken and Vegetables is now ready.

Thai Butternut Squash Soup with Chicken and Vegetables

by jmolineux
www.instructables.com/id/
Thai-Butternut-Squash-
Soup/

Step 1: Ingredients and Equipment

This is a recipe I learned at school. Please try it if you would like!

Ingredients you will need:

- 1 can of coconut milk (come mostly from Caribbean)
- 1 medium onion (come mostly from Spain)
- 1 medium butternut squash (come from either, Argentina, Istanbul, or South Africa)
- 1 jar or tub of red or green Thai curry paste (come from Thailand)
- 1 stock cube (Hint: Use any type apart from beef. This will make the soup extremely thick)
- 1 tablespoon of oil
- Thai basil to garnish (Hint: normal basil will also do)
- salt and pepper

Equipment you will need:

- pot
- measuring jug
- kettle
- stove/cooker
- blender or food processor
- tablespoon
- teaspoon
- butcher's knife
- wooden spoon
- potato or vegetable peeler

Step 2:

Chop the butternut squash into quarters and use the potato peeler to remove all the orange outer layer of skin. Chop into small pieces as the smaller the pieces are the quicker the butternut squash will take to soften before blending.

Step 3:

On the stove, place the pan on high heat and add one tablespoon of oil.

Chop the onion in half, dice into small chunks, and add to the pan.

Sweat the onions for 10 minutes, add a tablespoon of the

Thai green (or red) curry paste, and stir continuously for 2 minutes.

Step 4:

Boil the kettle and pour 100ml of water into the measuring jug.

Fill the measuring jug up to 200ml with cold water, and then pour 50ml out. This makes lukewarm water called tepid water.

Add the stock cube and stir continuously for a minute to make the stock.

Finally, add the butternut squash chunks, the coconut milk and the stock to the pan, then leave on a high temperature for 30–50 minutes (depending on how small the butternut squash chunks are and how long it takes for them to soften).

Get the blender or food processor ready.

When you feel the time is right, add some salt and pepper to the soup for seasoning, as much or little as you like. Don't put too much in though, as more can always be added later.

Step 5:

Tip the contents of the pan into the blender when the butternut squash is soft enough to purée. You may need to blend in batches if you have doubled the ingredients list to make more.

Season with more pepper (if you would like more) and when serving add the Thai basil (or basil) to the top of the soup bowl to garnish!

Et Voila! (and there you have it!) Your delightful, low fat Thai Butternut Squash Soup!

Tasty Dahl Soup

by Bindlestiff
www.instructables.com/id/
Delicious-Dahl-Soup/

Dahl Soup is one of those rare foods that is incredibly delicious and very healthy. It tastes as nourishing as a creamy soup but is less filling so you can eat more of it. It is exotic but made of easy-to-find ingredients. It is also quite forgiving; many of the ingredients can be substituted and many of the quantities can be adjusted. Hence it is a little different every time I make it, but it NEVER disappoints.

Not being a vegan, I can't imagine the agony of such an existence. But when I eat this vegan soup, I don't miss meat or dairy at all.

Step 1: Ingredients and Tools

- 1 teaspoon olive or sesame oil
- 1 chopped onion
- 2 cloves of garlic, chopped
- 2 cups vegetable stock or water
- 1 can of diced tomatoes
- 1 can of light coconut milk (or regular)
- 1 cup lentils (red are my favorite but other kinds will also work)
- 1 teaspoon cumin*
- 1 teaspoon coriander
- ¼ teaspoon cardamom
- ¼ teaspoon cinnamon
- 2 teaspoons ginger powder
- ¼ teaspoon cayenne pepper
- 1 teaspoon salt
- 2 teaspoons minced ginger
- 1 lemon
- bunch of chopped fresh cilantro (up to 1 cup chopped)

    *You can also use 1 teaspoon garam masala in place of the cumin, coriander, cardamom, and cinnamon.

You will also need:
- A large pot or Dutch oven
- A wooden spoon or paddle

tasty dahl soup

Step 2: Prep!
Prepping will make the process a lot smoother and enjoyable.
Before you turn on the stove:
1. Chop the onion and garlic
2. Measure all of the spices and salt into one container
3. Open the can of tomatoes and can of coconut milk
4. Chop the cilantro and cut the lemon in half

Step 3: Caramelize!
1. Heat the olive oil in your pot. I usually put the stove on "6"(out of 10), or medium high. Wait until the oil gets hot. I usually wait until I see a little bit of smoke rising from the pot. If the oil is not hot when you add the

onions, they will stick to the pan.
2. Add your onions and garlic and quickly stir them until they absorb some of the heat of the oil. Let them cook for about 6 minutes or until they are translucent. Stir them once in a while to make sure they don't stick or burn.

Step 4: Pile it in!
Add the remaining ingredients except for the lemon and cilantro.

(At this point I realized I didn't have quite enough lentils, so I added some quinoa, which turned out great.)

Let the liquids heat up to a simmer, then cover and reduce heat. Let the soup simmer for about twenty minutes or until the lentils are tender. Remove from heat.

When you are ready to serve the soup, add your chopped cilantro and then squeeze the lemon halves over it. Garnish with additional cilantro sprigs.

Eat it! This soup is also good reheated from the fridge or from frozen.

Carrot Soup

by syrrus

www.instructables.com/id/
Carrot-Soup/

Carrot Soup! Love soup? You'll love this one! Carrot soup is versatile, nutritious, and good on a warm summer day or cool winter evening.

Since this ible is for the hungry scientist contest, it'll have a healthy smattering of science in it. Bear with it, the science will help make you a better cook, and you'll soon be improvising, making additions and substitutions, and eyeballing ingredients in no time. By the by, I LOVE to cook, especially with a bunch of friends and a favorite beverage in hand. I recommend cooking this soup as part of a fall or winter meal with some friends; have them bring crusty bread, pungent cheese, and beverages.

Step 1: Ingredients

- 1 lb organic carrots
- 1 large baking potato
- 6–8 medium shallots
- 6 cloves garlic
- 1 bunch basil
- 2 tablespoons butter
- 1 teaspoon sugar
- several teaspoon salt
- several tsp pepper
- 1 teaspoon paprika
- 1 teaspoon coriander
- 1–2 teaspoons thyme
- 1–4 teaspoons cayenne pepper OR several whole dried chilies
- ¾–1 lb boneless skinless chicken breast
- 5 cups chicken stock
- 1 can coconut milk
- 1 cup heavy whipping cream
- A few stale dinner rolls, or any bread you have lying around

   *DO NOT UNDER ANY CIRCUMSTANCES BUY BABY CARROTS!!!!!! Baby carrots have a much higher sugar content than regular carrots do, and your soup will end up tasting really sweet and gross. If you skimp and cut corners on every other step, make sure you don't ignore this one.

Step 2: Prepping the Veggies

You want your veggies cut into pieces that will cook evenly during the browning process. The carrots should be peeled and cut into ¼ inch slices. The potatoes should be peeled and cut in half, then half again (see the pictures), then sliced into ¼-inch-thick slices. The shallots/onion should be peeled and sliced in half, then chopped into thin strips. Mince the garlic and basil.

When all of the veggies are prepared, put your stockpot onto the stove. Your stockpot doesn't have to be a real pot meant for soups, but it should be fairly large, have two sturdy handles so you can manage it, be tall (not strictly necessary, but helpful), and have a fairly thick bottom so it conducts heat well and evenly. Heat your pot for a minute or two on high heat, then add the butter until it is all melted but not burning. Add the veggies, and stir for a minute or two to combine everything evenly. Add your spices and stir again until combined evenly. At this point, you want to keep an eye on your pot, but you don't want to stir it constantly. If you do you'll never give the ingredients a chance to brown. Notice my pot isn't very large, so only some of my

veggies browned well. I like to use as few pots as I can (although I almost always fail at this), but you can use a larger pan for the browning, and then transfer everything into your stockpot. I personally love my cast iron pan. It's 12 inches in diameter, has a heavy bottom so it cooks evenly and holds heat well, and is generally awesome, but in the interest of dish parsimony, I decided to do everything in the stockpot.

Step 3: Chicken it Up!

The chicken will be cooked separately and added to the pot after everything else is done. Its purpose is to be something for you to chew on so you're not just slurping a liquid. It makes the soup much more satisfying, although it's not necessary.

Clean your chicken, and then slice it in half as if you were slicing two frozen hamburger patties that were stuck together (see the pictures). Now slice the halved breasts into ½-inch strips.

Move the chicken into a bowl; add the same spices you used on the veggies in smaller amounts. Eyeball this, I use about 1 teaspoon salt, 2 teaspoons ground pepper, 1 teaspoon paprika, 2 teaspoons cayenne pepper, 1 teaspoon dried basil, and a pinch or two of thyme. Add some oil (I like olive oil because of the flavor, and I have tons of it, but you might want to use a neutral oil that has a higher smoke point like canola. Toss the chicken.

Get out a frying pan. I have a sweet one I got in a free pile in my old apartment that has ridges, leaving room for air to circulate under the meat and giving "grill marks", but any frying pan will work as long as all of your chicken can contact the pan at once. Heat the pan on high heat, and when it is good and hot, spray it with cooking spray (or whatever you prefer: butter, oil, whatever). Add the chicken and cook for a few minutes (maybe 5 or so depending on the size of your pieces) until the

bottoms are white and the pieces are cooked half way through. Flip the pieces and cook until done through, flipping when you need to evenly brown all of the chicken on all sides (more or less).

Step 4: Making your Soup a Soup!

OK, so by now your veggies should be browned. If they aren't, keep cooking away. At a minimum everything should be cooked (no crunchy potatoes or carrots), if not browned.

Add the chicken stock and stir a few times. Add the can of coconut milk, and stir a few times to combine it. Pour in half the heavy whipping cream, and TASTE. Tasting is a very important part of cooking. You could have and should have been tasting the whole time, but it can be a little difficult to assess the seasoning of a soup by eating one hot carrot, so if you haven't tasted yet, defiantly do now. Add seasoning as needed for

your taste. A common pitfall of mine is seasoning to what I perceive to be other people's taste. This inevitably leads to a bland soup. Don't be afraid to add more spice, more salt, more pepper, whatever; just be sure to add in small increments so you don't over-spice. I usually end up adding the entire amount of cream, but you may prefer less, so add the second half slowly, stirring and tasting as you go. Remember, cream mutes flavors, so adding more cream might mean adding more pepper or salt or something else.

Now, add a few pieces of torn up bread. I added two dinner rolls I had lying around, but you may want less bread (or more. Who am I to tell you how to live your life?). Stir the soup every few minutes until the bread is soaked through and the whole concoction is barely boiling and small bubbles are forming around the sides of the pot

Step 5: Make It Creamy

So your soup is a soup now. It should taste Thai-esque and be delicious and can be served as it is, but the next bit takes it to the next level.

You need to purée your soup. My preferred way is to use a hand blender. They can be found for like $10 at a Goodwill. Mine has variable speeds, but it doesn't have to be fancy. If you don't want to use/ purchase a hand blender, a normal blender will work fine, just be sure to be safe about it. Your soup is very hot at this point, so if you purée it in a blender, the steam will escape very quickly and if your blender is overfull you will get soup shooting out the top. Only use a few cups of soup at a time, making sure to include enough liquid so everything blends smoothly. Hold a hand towel firmly over the top of the blender, and pulse until the chunks are much smaller, then hold on high until the soup is creamy. Transfer to a separate bowl and continue puréeing the soup in batches until it is all done. You can also use a food processer, but I've found mine didn't purée, it just made the pieces smaller (roughly several millimeters in diameter), but not puréed, and thus the texture was wrong.

Add the chunks of cooked chicken and stir to evenly distribute them in the soup. Taste one last time, re-season as needed, and take a bow, you've made yourself an awesome batch of carrot soup. I like to serve it with warmed crusty bread (like a take-n-bake baguette) and a beer, but it can be served as a first course or main course. A few pieces of chopped basil on top or some scallions sliced on the bais (diagonally) would be a nice touch if you're trying to impress your boss, but the flavor and texture speaks for itself, so unadulterated is fine too.

I hope you enjoy this soup as much as I do. You can chill it and serve it cool on a warm summer afternoon, or warm on a cold winter evening. You're a hungry scientist, experiment!

I'd like to give credit where credit is due. The original recipe came out of Mark Bitterman's *Best Recipes in the World*. The science came from lots of places, but probably mostly from Harold McGee's *On Food and Cooking*, and to a lesser extent Alton Brown's show *Good Eats*, and the bread chunks idea came from the *Cook's Illustrated* recipe for Creamy Tomato Soup.

awesome coconut milk recipes

White Gazpacho

by canida
www.instructables.com/id/
White-Gazpacho/

This is a slightly mutant form of the traditional white gazpacho, but still extremely tasty. Part of Black and White Day.

Step 1: Ingredients
- 1 cup almonds, blanched and skinned
- 1–8 cloves garlic (I used eight; you should probably start with one.)
- ½ tsp salt
- 1 large cucumber
- 2 cups sweet white fruit (Grapes, apples, pears, etc. I used Asian pears.)
- ¼ cup coconut milk
- ¼–½ cup cold water (Start with ¼, add more if necessary.)
- Salt and white pepper to taste

Step 2: Method
Pull out your food processor, and chop the almonds to powder.

Add the salt and garlic, and process until you have a crumbly paste.

Peel and chunk the cucumber and fruit, and add to the food processor.

Add coconut milk, process, and add cold water until you've reached a proper thick soupy consistency.

Add salt and white pepper to taste.

My food processor was actually too small for this (7c) so I switched to the blender. In that case, blend the cucumber and fruit with the coconut milk and enough water to make it go, and process until smooth. Add the nut and garlic paste. Adjust consistency with water, add salt and pepper to taste.

Step 3: Refrigerate
Serve cold or at room temperature.

Normally, white gazpacho would use white bread soaked in milk or water until soggy, and a bit of olive oil and possibly sherry. I chose to ignore that and go for more almonds and some coconut milk. I'd actually meant to include olive oil, but the coconut milk really took care of that niche.

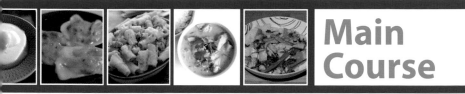

Main Course

Hawaiian Banana French Toast

by crapsoup
www.instructables.com/id/
Hawaian-Banana-French-
Toast/

Hawaiian Banana French Toast was my roommate's idea with a few of my own upgrades!

Step 1: Ingredients

- 1 full loaf of Hawaiian bread
- 3 eggs
- ½ cup coconut milk
- ¼ teaspoon vanilla
- ½ banana (or the full banana if you really like bananas)
- 1 teaspoon cinnamon
- 2 tablespoons oil (and more if needed)

Step 2: Instructions

- Purée ½ of banana in food processor or mash in small bowl until relatively smooth.
- Mix eggs, milk, banana purée, vanilla, and cinnamon in dipping tray.
- Cut crust off of the sides of the bread.
- Cut bread into slices about 1 inch thick
- Cut all the slices in half. Eat or discard crust.
- Heat oil in frying pan on medium heat.
- Place slices into egg mix, coating all sides thoroughly.
- Fry both sides in pan until golden brown, about 1 to 2 minutes each side.
- Serve warm with butter and syrup, and maybe even peanut butter if you're into that kind of thing.

Vegan Egg
by belsey
www.instructables.com/id/
Vegan-Egg/

Vegans won't eat or use animal products—so the whole idea of a vegan egg is oxymoronic, a contra-diction of terms, an impossibility, right?

Wrong!

I will show you in this instructable how to cook up a vegan sunny-side up egg that contains no animal products. It looks like an egg, it feels like an egg, but no bird ever laid eyes on this baby.

This is not the easiest recipe to follow. It requires a fair amount of specialized and hard to find ingredients, but once you've gathered everything you need, and you've practiced a few times, it's fairly quick, very tasty (it's a desert), and super fun to serve. This is extreme gastronomy, cooking for the concept, deconstructing the age old question of (which comes first) the chicken or the egg and replacing it with the more fundamental question: what is an egg?

Step 1: Ingredients and Materials

The main ingredients are mangos, coconut milk, and sugar, with a little bit of rice flour. Coconut milk is sold in 16oz cans and you can buy it either sweetened or unsweetened, low fat or regular. I used the unsweetened full fat variety. It should work with any kind (just don't add extra sugar if you buy the sweetened variety).

You will also need calcium lactate and sodium alginate (to give your egg yolk the right shape and texture) and agar for the egg white. Sodium alginate and agar are extracted from seaweed, and calcium lactate, despite its name, is NOT made from milk (it is made by reacting lactic acid with calcium carbonate. Lactic acid, in turn is made with sugar, water, and chalk). This desert is 100 percent vegan fun.

For tools you will need a hand blender and a small slotted spoon.

Although you might be able to find the ingredients locally and individually, it is much easier to buy a kit online. ThinkGeek carries a kit made by moleculeR, which is fairly expensive but has very pretty packaging, and it's convenient because you'll get a good sample of ingredients and all the specialized tools too. It is from their DVD that I got the idea for this recipe: they give instructions for a reconstructed egg, but they didn't take the concept to its logical conclusion, they didn't make it vegan. Their egg white is made with regular milk and doesn't taste as good as this version. Another online vendor is The Spice House which carries all three "molecular" ingredients, sodium alginate, calcium lactate, and agar.

Step 2: Preparation

Chill 6 small individual serving plates in your freezer.

Use your hand blender to dissolve 2 grams of sodium alginate (about ¾ of a teaspoon) in 2 cups of water, and then refrigerate it for 15–30 minutes.

Step 3: Mix Egg Whites Together

- 3 tablespoons sugar (omit if you are using sweetened coconut milk)
- ½ teaspoon agar (2 grams)
- 1 tablespoon rice flour
- 1 pinch salt

Sift the sugar mix into ½ cup coconut milk, stirring carefully to avoid clumps. Bring to a boil over moderate heat in a small saucepan.

Stir in an additional cup of coconut milk, and remove from heat.

Set out your chilled plates, and pour about 3 tablespoons of "egg white" onto each plate. You should have about ¼ cup left in your pan after serving all six plates. Put saucepan with remaining coconut mix over low heat and wait a couple minutes for the first layer of "egg white" to set.

When the first layer is hard enough to support an extra layer, spoon the remaining coconut sauce over the gelled "egg white" on each plate. You may have to add extra coconut milk before pouring if the mix has thickened too much.

Allow to set about 5 minutes (in the refrigerator if you've got the space, but it will also work at room temperature).

If you are preparing this dish a few hours or even a day in advance, after the egg white is set you can pour a little coconut milk (diluted with water if necessary) over the egg whites, cover and store in the refrigerator.

Step 4: Egg Yolks

Peel and cube one large, ripe mango or 2 small "champagne" mangos. If you can find the Champagne mangos, these are much better, not just for this recipe but for all purposes: they are sweeter and less fibrous than any other variety. There are whole instructables devoted to the subject of cutting mangos, but these instructions are best suited for my recipe.

Blend together:
- Mango
- ½ teaspoon calcium lactate

- 1–2 tablespoons sugar (depending on your taste and how ripe and sweet your mangos are)

Remove the sodium alginate bath from the fridge and pour into a shallow bowl so the mixture comes close to the rim (this will make your job easier)

Prepare a second bowl filled with clean water nearby, and,if you are preparing this in advance, a third container with about 1 cup of mango juice.

Use a soup spoon to carefully drop a dollop (about ½ to ¾ tablespoon) of the mango purée into the sodium alginate bath. You can put in 2 or maybe 3 dollops at a time, as long as you are careful not to let them touch each other. It is very hard to get a perfect sphere but don't worry, once it's on your egg it will look fine.

Use your slotted spoon to (very gently) mix the solution around the yolks so an even gel forms around each one. Leave in the bath at least 3 minutes, then, with your slotted spoon, pick them up one at a time and rinse them in your bowl of water. If you are serving immediately, proceed to step 5, otherwise after rinsing the yolks place them in some mango juice to store in the refrigerator until you are ready to serve. You can put them in water instead of juice, but depending on how long you are storing them, they will absorb some of the liquid. In water (overnight) the taste will become a bit diluted and the texture more liquid, less gooey.

Step 5: Assembly

If you prepared some parts in advance, carefully pour the liquid off the egg whites and wipe the plates dry. Presentation is everything here!

Using your slotted spoon, carefully lift the yolks out of the mango juice, rinse them in a bowl of fresh water and place them on the center of the second layer of egg white.

Play around with this recipe. Next time I make these I'll use a little food coloring on the yolk to make some green eggs and ham. Maybe I'll color the egg whites too and serve rainbow eggs...but this time around I was going for the 100 percent realistic look.

This is a decently quick meal that tastes great and reheats like a dream!

Step 1: Ingredients for the Main Dish

- 2 cups rice
- 2 cups coconut milk (if your can of coconut milk does not equal 2 cups just make up the needed amount in water)
- 1 can bean sprouts
- 1 can bamboo shoots

- 3–5 chicken thighs (This is dark meat which doesn't dry out like white meat during the frying.) If you prefer white meat, then 2–4 chicken breasts should do the trick.
- veggies (This is really up to you, we do snow peas, water chestnuts, broccoli, cabbage, green beans . . . etc.)

Sauce: (Best Part)

- 1.5 cups orange marmalade (look for the "all natural" kind to stay away from HFCS)
- 5 tablespoons soy sauce (make sure it's La Choy or similar brand that doesn't use wheat in the sauce)
- 5 teaspoons of Sriracha (or more if you like spicy) This amount will be well over what you need but keep in the fridge for anything else that needs a little orange kick!

Step 2: Prepare

Put a small amount of cooking oil in one skillet and start warming it up. While the oil is warming, trim the chicken and cut into bite size pieces

About half way through prepping the chicken, wash your hands and start a larger skillet with all of your fresh (or frozen) veggies. Go back to trimming.

After you've started frying the chicken, start the rice.

Rice:

Prepare as package indicates. We use coconut milk instead of water . . . or half-and-half.

Step 3: Orange Sauce

BEST PART! . . . Take the ingredients mentioned in step 1 and whisk together in large measuring cup. Using the measuring cup will help you calculate the amount of soy sauce and Sriracha you might need to add if you use a jar of orange marmalade that has more or less than 1.5 cups.

To recalculate, here is a small break down; ¼ cup of orange marmalade plus 1 tablespoon soy sauce and 1 teaspoon Sriracha. (I use a little less soy lately and a little more Sriracha.)

Step 4: Plate and Eat

After your chicken has reached the proper temp and the rice and veggies are all cooked up nice, plate any way you would like and get the sauce a-flowing.

Step 5: Bonus Condiment

Dynamite Sauce—Good Good Good!

Ingredients:

- ½ cup REAL Mayonnaise
- 2 tablespoons Sriracha
- ¼ teaspoon Sesame Seed Oil

Mix the ingredients together, ENJOY!

**Great with left over rice from any meal.

I love coconut-based Indian curries and decided to try making one at home. It turns out to be ridiculously easy, and absolutely delicious!

In this case I've used chunks of leftover lamb (cooked sous vide by ewilhelm for our potluck) but you could also use chicken, fish, shrimp, tofu, or whatever you're excited about. I'm going to start making this sauce by the bucket load and adding whatever previously-cooked meat we have on hand. The important part is using pre-cooked meat (or seafood that cooks very quickly) for maximum speed and tastiness.

Step 1: Onions and Curry

Finely chop two medium onions and sauté in about 2–3 tablespoons of coconut oil and ½ teaspoon salt until onion is soft. (You can sub butter or the fat of your choice, but coconut oil increases the coconutty flavor!)

Add 2 tablespoons of your favorite curry powder and stir until thoroughly mixed. If it starts to stick or burn, add more fat.

Using a microplane grater, grate in two cloves of garlic. Stir in with the rest of the onion/curry/oil paste.

Step 2: Add Coconut Milk and Meat

Add one can full-fat coconut milk, stir, and simmer on low heat for about 5–10 minutes to allow flavors to mingle. Taste and adjust seasonings. If it's watery, cook down for a few more minutes, and then add the lamb.

Since the lamb is already cooked, you're just simmering long enough to dry the curry a bit more, and make sure all the amazing flavors penetrate the meat. This should take around 5 minutes.

If you like, this is the time to add golden raisins (sultanas), cashews, cilantro, or any other interesting chunks you'd like in your curry.

Step 3: Serve

That's it. Really. Serve over rice if you like, or just eat with a spoon. Like all curries, it tastes even better the next day, if you can wait that long.

This was one of the best curries I've ever had, as well as one of the fastest to make! The real trick is in using pre-cooked lamb—it was perfectly tender from cooking 24 hours sous vide, and was just simmered long enough to pick up the amazing curry flavors without becoming tough or dry. The smell wafted out through Pier 9, and we gave out plenty of samples in the test kitchen—everyone gave this curry rave reviews.

Try it, and tell me how it goes!

This is one of the tastiest and flavorsome curries I've ever made.

The curry has an amazingly fresh taste, with creamy coconut, just enough chili and loads of coriander.

The original recipe excluded the vegetables, but because I had a house full of students I added vegetables I thought would complement it to help fill us up and make it cheaper. If you don't fancy green beans, mange tout go really well as well.

The recipe for the curry paste I use can be found here. It's really quick to make in batches in a food processor and can be frozen up to 6 months for convenience.

Step 1: Ingredients

- 2 tablespoons green thai curry paste (according to taste)
- 1 tablespoon soft dark brown sugar
- 2–3 large carrots, cut into thin sticks
- 200g fine green beans, cut into 4-cm lengths
- 1–2 thick stalks lemongrass, fat ends bashed with a rolling pin (optional), I use paste
- 750g or 1½ lbs skinless, boneless chicken, cut into chunks (use breast and/or leg meat)
- zest and juice of one lime
- 400ml/14fl oz coconut milk (a can full)
- 2 tablespoons Thai fish sauce (or light soy sauce)
- handful of coriander, roughly chopped (the more the better though to be honest)

green thai chicken curry

fry with the chicken for a further 5 minutes on a medium heat. This helps them soak up the flavors from the paste.

If you like your curries hot now would be a good time to add an extra chili. The chilies in the paste are usually plenty for me though. I think this curry is more about the flavors than the heat.

Step 2: Fry the Chicken in the Paste

Add the paste to a large pan. If frozen, heat until it melts.

Heat the paste until it starts to fry, allow it to do so for a few minutes. Then throw in the chicken.

Fry the chicken in the paste on a medium heat for 5 minutes.

Step 4: In With the Rest

Finally, add the fish sauce, lemongrass, lime, coconut milk, and coriander. Allow to simmer gently until the carrots and beans are cooked to your liking.

Serve with rice. Yum!

Step 3: Add the Veggies

Lop the ends of the beans and carrots. Cut the beans in half and chop the carrots into thin sticks.

Add the soft brown sugar to the pan. Drop in the vegetables and

Shredded Sweet Potato Pancakes with Coconut Milk

by ewilhelm
www.instructables.com/id/
Shredded-Sweet-Potato-
Pancakes-with-Coconut-
Milk/

Sweet potato pancakes taste great, and the coconut milk gives them a subtle yet exotic flavor that's a lot of fun. They're also perfect for Orange Day.

I used a recipe from Whole Foods as a base, because its addition of coconut milk really appealed to me: Sweet Potato Pancakes with Ricotta Cheese (we skipped the cheese).

Ingredients:
- 2 medium sweet potatoes or yams, peeled and shredded by food processor (about 4 cups)
- a handful of pre-peeled garlic cloves, chopped in a food processor
- 1 medium yellow onion, chopped in a food processor
- 2 tablespoons flour
- about a teaspoon sea salt
- about a teaspoon of white pepper
- about a teaspoon dried basil and oregano

- 3 large eggs, lightly beaten
- 3 tablespoons coconut oil

Recipe:
Place everything in a large bowl and mix until egg completely coats the sweet potatoes.

Heat some canola oil (refined for high heat) in a large skillet or griddle. Working in batches, and using more oil as needed, use ½ cups sweet potato batter to make each pancake.

Cook, covered, for 5 minutes on each side, or until lightly browned. Remove to a platter and serve immediately.

Turn on your orange playlist, plate with other orange foods, and eat while wearing your most vibrantly orange gear. Matches well with the Instructables color scheme.

Notes: I made six pancakes to start, got fed up with separating and flipping them, and so just dumped the remaining potatoes on the griddle and cooked them like hash browns.

When I make this dish again, I'll microwave the shredded sweet potatoes for about a minute before mixing them with the rest of the ingredients. The potatoes started to brown slightly before they were cooked all the way through. Pre-cooking in the microwave will make them perfect.

shredded sweet potato pancakes with coconut milk

Satay Chicken
by Aadencash
www.instructables.com/id/
Satay-Chicken/

The peanut butter can be excluded if you have a peanut butter allergy. It should still taste great.

This goes great with rice so if you are thinking of that then a good idea would be to cook the rice as you prepare this dish since it doesn't take too long to prepare.

Step 1: Harvest your Ingredients

Ingredients

- 3 boneless chicken breasts
- cooking oil (not pictured)
- onions
- sweet chili sauce
- oyster sauce
- minced garlic
- ginger
- coconut milk
- Peanut butter (not pictured)

NOTE: I personally prefer the Panda Brand Oyster Sauce but any Oyster Sauce should do. They do taste different however, so you may want to experiment a little first. All these ingredients should be in your local grocery store (the Sweet Chili Sauce and Oyster Sauce should be in your Asian section. If your store has no Asian section maybe you can ask an Asian friend. If you have no Asian friends, then make an Asian friend).

Step 2: Cut Up Chicken and Onion

Cut the chicken breast into bite size chunks.

For 3 chicken breasts, one clove of onion is enough. However, it is really up to your taste. Some people love a ton of onions and I've eaten it that way before and it tastes fine. I haven't tried it without onions though.

Step 3: Adding Chicken and Onions

Set the stove to medium high to high heat.

Add 2 tablespoons of oil.

Add the chicken. You will want to make sure the chicken is cooked all the way through before you proceed to the next step because once you add the oyster sauce in, it will be hard to tell if the chicken is cooked. Make sure the chicken has turned color and if you need to, cut a few in half to see if they're cooked on the inside.

Add the onions.

Note: you should start seeing a lot of water boiling out. Don't worry about that. It should actually work to keep the food from drying out completely.

Step 4: The Sauces

Set the stove to medium heat.
Add ¾ cup of oyster sauce.
Add ¾ cup of sweet chili sauce.
Stir the pot until it is evened out.

Step 5: The Spices

Add 2 teaspoons of minced garlic.
Add a dash of ginger.
Stir.

Step 6: The Extra Touch

Add one tablespoon of coconut milk. You want to make sure the coconut milk is complimentary to the dish and that it doesn't overpower the other tastes (unless of course, you like it that way).

Add one teaspoon of peanut butter and stir.

Let the whole thing cook for a minute longer.

Taste test it. You should be able to taste every ingredient.

Step 7: The Dish

And there you have it. Enjoy.
Or if it tastes weird, try try again.

Upside-Down Persimmon Pancakes

by savynaturalista
www.instructables.com/id/
Upside-Down-Persimmon-
Pancakes/

Ingredients:

- 1.5 cups all-purpose flour
- 3½ tsps. baking powder
- 1 tsp salt
- 1¼ cups coconut milk
- 1 egg
- 3 tbsps. butter (melted)
- 2 cups fuyu persimmons (diced)

Recipe:

On medium heat place a skillet with a small amount of oil and let warm up. In a large bowl sift dry ingredients, and add egg and milk and pour in melted butter quickly stirring so the butter does not firm up. Let batter settle for a few minutes; pour batter in skillet and add a few diced persimmons. Flip the pancakes after a few seconds and let cook on the other side. Once done serve with butter, warm maple syrup, or honey.

Pasta Al Forno
by savynaturalista
www.instructables.com/id/
Pasta-Al-Forno-Baked-Ziti/

Ingredients:
- 16 oz cooked rigatoni (al dente)
- 3 cups cooked chicken breast (I used leftovers)
- 2 cups pumpkin purée
- 1 can of coconut milk
- 1 teaspoon salt
- black pepper and salt (to taste)
- 1 tablespoon nutritional yeast (optional)
- 1 teaspoon dry mustard
- 2 teaspoons thyme (dry or fresh)

Recipe:
Preheat oven to 375 degrees. Shred chicken and set aside. Place cooked pasta and chicken in a large bowl and mix. In the food processor, add coconut milk, pumpkin purée, nutritional yeast, thyme and 1 tsp. of salt; blending until all the ingredients are creamy. Place pumpkin sauce over the pasta and chicken, add salt and pepper to taste. Stir well making sure the pasta and chicken are coated. Place pasta in a casserole or baking dish and let bake for 10–20 minutes. Serve warm.

Massaman Curry

by jessyratfink
www.instructables.com/id/
massaman-curry/

Massaman curry is one of my new favorite meals. I had it for the first time a couple years ago when I came to be an artist in residence at Instructables, and I knew right away I had to figure out how to make it. I just love the smell of massaman curry—the ginger and lemongrass—and how creamy but spicy it is. It's definitely a very intricately seasoned dish—the layers of flavor are unlike nothing else.

Over the past six months or so, I've been messing with it and now it tastes just like the massaman curry at the Thai place I order it from.

I've tried it with chicken, beef, and tofu—I don't know that I can fully recommend the tofu in it, but chicken and beef were super tasty.

Step 1: Ingredients

- one pound beef, chicken, or pork (or tofu, if you insist)
- one pound potatoes
- 1 onion, diced
- 1 two inch long piece of ginger, grated
- 4–5 cloves garlic, grated or minced
- 2 teaspoons plus chili garlic paste (I use 4-5)
- 14 oz can broth to match meat/tofu choice
- 14 oz can coconut milk
- 1 stalk lemongrass, minced
- 3 bay leaves
- 1½ teaspoons turmeric
- 1 teaspoon ground coriander
- 1 teaspoon whole cumin seed
- ½ teaspoon pepper
- ¼ teaspoon cardamon
- 1 teaspoon tamarind
- ½–1 tablespoons fish sauce
- ½ tablespoon brown sugar

I know this list is a little overwhelming, but many of these ingredients are great staples to have around. I've worked really hard to get it to taste just right, so I can't promise it will taste the same if you leave something out or substitute. This is one of the only times I stress actually using the recipe.

Also, go easy on the fish sauce. I always use ½ tablespoon because I'm not fond of it, and I feel like it overpowers the other flavors.

Depending on the meat you choose, your cooking times will vary. More on that in step 5.

until soft and fragrant. Then add in the turmeric, cardamom, cumin seeds, coriander, black pepper, bay leaves, and tamarind paste. Stir this around until everything smells amazing and is colored orange.

Step 2: Prep

Cut your meat/tofu and potatoes into bite size chunks.

Mince you lemongrass (and save about a tablespoon to put in near the end of cooking!) and dice your onion. Peel the onion and garlic—you can either mince it or grate it directly into the pan.

You can also measure out your spices to make the next step quicker.

Step 3: Sautéing

Pop a bit of oil (use coconut if you've got it!) into the bottom of a large pot and heat over medium.

Add in the onion, lemongrass, ginger, and garlic and stir it around

Step 4: Add the Meat, Potatoes, and Liquids

Add in the stock and then your potatoes and chicken. Stir this around really well and scrape all the yummy bits off the bottom of the pot.

Then add in the coconut milk and stir again.

Step 5: Simmering

This is a long simmering dish. You want to take it low and slow so the flavors develop, the potatoes cook, and your meats/tofu are well flavored and soft. Here are the approximate cook times for the various meats/tofu if you want them to be delicious and tender:

Chicken—1 hour

tofu—1 hour

pork—1–2 hours

beef—2–3 hours (yeah, for real, it took that long)

You can definitely cut the time and say screw it if you don't mind chewy meat.

My recommendation is to simmer with the lid slightly cracked—that way you're reducing the liquid little by little and intensifying the flavors.

In the last 15 minutes or so of cooking, I like to add in the reserved lemongrass to give it an extra kick of flavor. The lemongrass can get a little subtle after cooking for a long time.

Once it's thickened to your liking and the meat is nice and tender, pull it off the heat and serve with rice. I like jasmine, but I bet any type will be tasty with it!

Creamy Chicken Pasta—Mouth Watering

by shazni
www.instructables.com/id/
Chicken-Pasta-Mouth-
Watering/

I first ate this at my husband's aunt's house and found it delicious! What was even great was my kids, who are very very fussy eaters, loved it. So I asked her and tried it, it was delicious. My mom and sisters tried it and they wanted the recipe too!.

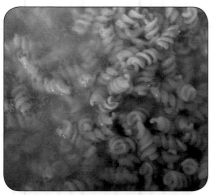

Step 1: Ingredients

- pasta—A must!
- cinnamon
- karapincha—an herb for the smell . . . it's optional. . .you can skip it. (I currently don't know the English name for it . . . but it's great for cholesterol/diabetes.)
- cardamom pods
- cumin seeds—2 tsp ground
- green chili—15—grind it, but not too much
- ginger and garlic paste—to make your own simply grind 100g of garlic, 50 grams of ginger and 1.5 teaspoons of olive oil (oil is optional)
- onions finely chopped
- 4 big tomatoes chopped
- chopped chicken—boiled with salt and pepper and then chopped . . . keep the bones . . . it's tasty!
- salt to taste
- coconut milk—1 cup thick and 2 cups thin milk (you could use pasteurized milk as a substitute)
- vegetable oil

Step 2: Grind, Boil, Chop!

Boil the chicken with salt and pepper and then cut into small pieces.

Boil pasta ¾ of the way done . . . but not fully and drain.

Grind chili. If you like a bit of pieces, don't grind totally. If you did, no problem, it won't make a difference in taste.

Grind the cumin seeds.

Chop onions and tomatoes finely.

Powder the cardamom pods, or just smash them.

Get your milk ready—Pasteurized milk/desiccated coconut powder or the real thing.

Step 3: Now Cook It!

Heat 2 tablespoons of oil

Add 2 tablespoons of ginger and garlic paste, then karapincha (herb-optional), cinnamon, onions, cumin seeds.

Cook a bit, now add the tomatoes, and then the green chili and salt to taste.

Add the chicken, then the thin milk, and then the thick milk. Mix, now add the pasta, sprinkle the cardamom and mix and let simmer for 5 min. (This is why I said boil pasta ¾ of the way.)

Once you are done, grab a plate and heap it with pasta and enjoy your meal!

Dutch Oven Thai Curry Noodles

by 3leftturns
www.instructables.com/id/
Dutch-Oven-Thai-Curry-
Noodles/

- long handled metal tongs (for moving charcoal)
- shovel
- trivet/lid stand
- lid lifter (claw hammer works really well)
- heat resistant gloves
- apron
- something to put the oven on. When I started I used tinfoil, then a $1 pizza pan. I now use the Volcano cooker.
- flat edged wooden spoon with the longest handle you can find.
- charcoal
- lighter fluid
- matches

Some nice extras:
- charcoal chimney
- waist height table
- propane burner stove
- dinner triangle

Dutch oven cooking is easy, but a lot of people worry too much about technique, coal counting, and overhead costs. Not only can it be easy, it can also be cheap. I love Dutch oven cooking so much, I fire up the charcoal and cook in my ovens every weekend. You can read about my adventures on my blog, the Back Porch Gourmet. Getting started is easy, and this instructable will teach you how to make my favorite food—Curry!

Step 1: You Will Need

To do Dutch oven cooking in general, you will need a few tools. I recommend the following list for beginners:
- 12" seasoned cast iron Dutch oven (read my squidoo lens on seasoning cast iron)

Step 2: Ingredients
- oil
- rice noodles
- chicken breast
- curry powder
- ginger powder
- paprika
- 1 can coconut milk
- sliced mushrooms
- bell pepper, sliced
- love

Garnish:
- sriracha
- garlic
- chili sauce

Step 3: Light the Fire
Fill the chimney half full of charcoal—as a general rule, I fill the chimney half full if I am cooking one dish, and all the way for up to three. Soak the coals with a little lighter fluid and throw in a match. Go inside and prepare the food.

The coals will be ready when embers glow and little flames stick in between the charcoal. The fire will go out, so don't worry; it is still working. Now and then you will see smoke rising from the chimney, and as they say, "Where there's smoke, there's fire."

Step 4: Soak the Noodles
Pull the noodles out of the package, ½ for 4 servings, all of it for 8. Get your tap water running very hot and fill a bowl with water. Submerge the noodles and finagle them until they are completely immersed. If they are not all submerged, they will not cook evenly.

Rice noodles are made from rice flour, which is essentially ground up rice. Merely soaking the noodles in hot water softens them and they are edible. I love working with these noodles.

Step 5: Cut the Meat and Vegetables
Cut the chicken into thin strips across the grain. If you are using chicken breasts, this is generally across the smallest point. Using a different knife and cutting board,

slice the bell pepper. If you are cooking for 4, cut one of each; up to 8, cut two. If your mushrooms are not presliced, slice them.

By now, the coals should be ready. Take your ingredients in bowls outside.

Step 6: Prepare the Dutch Oven

Using the tongs, move the charcoal to the cooking surface, whether it be a $1 cookie sheet or the fanciest Dutch oven table. It doesn't really matter. Spread out the coals evenly and hold your hand above, looking for hotspots. Adjust charcoal accordingly.

For this meal, I started with 12, but ended up using 15. If you

don't have the shielding that the Volcano offers, use a few more. For baking at 350 degrees, a good rule of thumb is to take the diameter (often printed on the lid) and add 3 to that number. That is how many to stack on top. Subtract 3 from the diameter, and that is how many to add to the bottom.

Place the Dutch oven on the coals and add some oil. It doesn't have to be too much—I used about a quarter cup and it worked great. Let the oil heat up. To tell when it is ready, flick some clean water from your fingers into the oven. If it sizzles and sputters, you are ready.

Step 7: Add the Meat and Spices

Add the chicken strips and shake in the spices. I don't have amounts, but be generous. You can spice it as spicy as you like. When I added the coconut milk in step 9, I opened the wrong end of the curry and added a lot. It still tasted good. Be generous with the spices, the coconut milk will calm them down.

Stir the chicken until cooked completely with the flat edged spoon. The flat edge allows you to scrape the bottom, keeping things from burning.

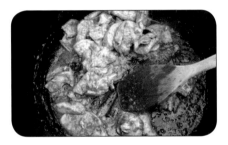

Step 8: Add the Vegetables

Add the vegetables—peppers and mushrooms. We want them to cook, but still keep some crispness. You'll know they are done when they just start to turn clear. Stir often with the spoon.

Step 9: Add the Noodles and Coconut Milk

Add the soaked noodles and coconut milk. Stir, adding any additional spices. If you want it spicy, add a little garlic chili sauce or Sriracha sauce at this point. Boil for only a few minutes, just to heat up the noodles.

Step 10: Enjoy!

Plate it up and offer your guests some garnish—Asian hot sauces, soy sauce, limes, and cilantro.

To clean up, scrape any remaining food preferably when the oven is still hot and wash out any food with water. DO NOT USE SOAP! Soap will decay the protective patina. Wipe clean and store with a paper towel in the oven, with the lid propped open a little. If you're concerned about germs, you can heat up the iron to kill any bacteria and add a little oil with a basting brush. Don't add a big coat of oil, and don't add any if you are not heating the iron. Leaving a coating of oil on the cast iron will just go rancid and make a sticky goo that will be hard to remove.

Dispose of the fire safely, dropping coals into a bucket of water is not only safe, it's pretty cool to watch. They float until they go out and then they sink. They really sizzle!

Sweet Potato Ravioli with Coconut Curry Sauce

by RollerScrapper
www.instructables.com/id/
Sweet-Potato-Ravioli-with-
Coconut-
Curry-Sauce/

This instructable shows you how to create your own ravioli by using won ton wrappers and crimping them with a cookie cutter. This technique can be done for any flavor of ravioli with your favorite sauce, but here's a flavor combo I dreamed up while thinking of the pasta contest.

The combo is great, the sweet potato is complemented at first by the sweet of the sauce and is followed by a lovely fragrant curry and spice.

This recipe is also vegan. I am not vegan or vegetarian, but believe me, you don't miss the meat or cheese here, as the sweet potato and the curry take center stage.

Step 1: Ingredients For the Ravioli

- Won Ton Wrappers, buy the thickest ones you can find. I got mine at the Asian grocery store
- Trader Joe's Roasted Mashed Sweet Potato

Note, these cooking amounts are approximate. This is where you can just use your eye and keep tasting to create a sauce that is sweet and spicy to your taste.

For the Sauce:
- ⅔ cup coconut milk
- 1 tablespoon curry
- a few shakes of red pepper flakes
- 1 teaspoon soy sauce
- 1 teaspoon black vinegar
- a few shakes of garlic salt
- pepper to taste
- 2 tablespoons brown sugar
- 1 teaspoon sesame seed oil
- 3 tablespoons corn starch
- water

Step 2: Start Making the Ravioli

Lay out some won ton skins.

Nuke 2 of the sweet potato "pucks" at a time for about 20 seconds.

Put half of a puck worth of sweet potato on the skin and use your fingers to put some warm water around it.

Seal the second wonton skin on top.

Now if you're not into cute ravioli, you can stop here, this makes a fine ravioli. But I wanted to go a step further and make Hello Kitty ravioli, so if you're into cute, go to the next step.

Step 3: Make the Ravioli Cute

Using a cookie cutter, cut out the shape. This also helps seal the edges.

When you're done cutting, you can use your fingers to squeeze the edges sealed even better, before laying it on a tray to rest.

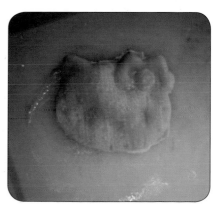

Step 4: Cooking the Sauce and Ravioli

Start a pot of boiling water on your back burner.

On the front burner combine the following:

- ⅔ cup coconut milk
- 1 tablespoon curry
- a few shakes of red pepper flakes
- 1 teaspoon soy sauce
- 1 teaspoon black vinegar
- a few shakes of garlic salt
- pepper to taste
- 2 tablespoons brown sugar
- 1 teaspoon sesame seed oil

Next, combine in a measuring cup 3 tablespoons corn starch and water.

While the sauce heats up, fully mix your corn starch mixture and slowly pour it into the sauce, while stirring. The heat and the cornstarch will quickly thicken the sauce. You won't need that entire amount of cornstarch necessarily, so stop when you get a thick enough sauce to your taste. If you over add, you can add in some more coconut milk to thin it out a bit. I did that and then added in another shake of garlic salt to take the sweetness down a notch.

When your sauce is done you can turn off the heat and start cooking your ravioli.

Using a slotted spoon gently put your ravioli into the boiling water. Do a maximum of 6 in a pot, but make sure to put in one, and gently stir, and then add the next one, so they don't all stick together, or to the bottom of the pot. Cook for 3 minutes. The reason for the max of 6 is that your ravioli will slow the boil down. Since they cook so quickly it's no big deal to do several batches.

Once they're done, use a slotted spoon to gently remove them and drain out the water.

Step 5: Plate and Enjoy!

I like to put a base of sauce on my plate, then about 3 ravioli, and put more sauce on top.

This is an incredibly flavorful sauce so you do not want to put on too much or it will overwhelm the ravioli.

Chef's notes: While you could actually fit a frozen sweet potato puck into a circular ravioli if you are not going to use a cookie cutter, I don't recommend it. I tried that first and the amount of sweet potato was not a good ratio to that of the pasta and the sauce. It certainly is easier, but for me, it was too much sweet potato.

Enjoy your Hello Kitty Shaped Sweet Potato Ravioli with Coconut Curry Sauce!

Chipotle Coconut Creamed Corn

by canida
www.instructables.com/id/
Chipotle-Coconut-Creamed-
Corn/

A savory blend of disparate food traditions. Or, cleaning out the fridge.

Step 1: Acquire and Prep Ingredients

It's summer, and that means fresh corn. I'm a complete corn snob, but also an optimist—I buy corn at the farmers' market, always hoping that one day it will actually be up to the standards I'm used to. I grew up eating great corn in Indiana, and even got fantastic corn in Boston—I followed Stillman's Farm to just about every farmers' market in the city when their Mirai corn was in season. Surprisingly, I've completely failed to find very good corn in California—we keep trying, but after an ear or two eaten straight, we end up cutting the corn off the cob for use as an ingredient. **Thus, you'll need:**

- 5–8 ears fresh sweet corn on the cob
- 1 large onion
- 1 bunch basil (parsley or cilantro can substitute; it just has to be fresh)
- 1 bunch scallions
- ½ cup coconut milk or coconut cream
- 2 tablespoons chipotle peppers in adobo sauce (from a can)
- sugar (maybe)
- salt and pepper

Shuck the corn, and cut the kernels off the cob with a very sharp knife. I just got this OXO Corn Stripper from Williams-Sonoma, and I am quite happy with it. It's easy to use, and there's much less mess from kamikaze corn kernels. Even my mom liked it.

Chop the onion into small chunks, about the same size as the corn kernels. Chop the scallions, basil, and chipotles.

Step 2: Sauté Onions and Corn

Preheat a large pot, and then melt a pat of butter with some oil.

Add the corn and onion to the pot, and stir until the onion becomes translucent.

Step 3: Add Remaining Ingredients

Add the chipotles, scallions, and coconut cream, and half of the fresh herbs. Cook approximately 10 minutes until the corn has softened, and the coconut milk has picked up the color and flavors from the rest of the ingredients.

Season to taste with salt and pepper, then stir in the remaining fresh herbs. If the corn isn't sweet enough on its own, add a bit of sugar to punch it up. This is especially relevant if the corn is old, as the sugars turn to starch over time.

Step 4: Serve

Serve warm or cold.

The flavors mingle and deepen after overnight refrigeration, but double-check the seasonings again before serving the corn cold.

This works beautifully as a side dish with grilled meats and is a fantastic base for corn-and-peach salsa.

This is about the tastiest Thai dish I can make. I try to order it often from different restaurants around town (Nakhon Ratchasima) to see what people are putting in, and I have come up with my own vegetarian ultra-delicious version.

Enjoy!

Step 1: Gather Ye Ingredients!

The 2 main ingredients are winged beans and nam prik pao, which is a type of chili paste made with roasted chilies and sour tamarind.

Outside of Thailand, these 2 ingredients may be hard to find, so I've included substitutions here to let you still amaze people with the breadth of your culinary skills.

There are a few ingredients, but nothing too complicated!

You're gonna need:

- 1 large egg
- ½ kilo winged beans (tua ploo) (substitute: ½ kilo fresh greenbeans, snowpeas, and/or carrots)
- 2 tablespoons vegetable oil
- 1 cup coconut milk
- ½ cup peanuts (shelled, skinned)
- 1 large clove garlic
- 1 small handful of shallots
- ½ lime
- dry and fresh chilies
- sugar
- vinegar
- seasoned soy sauce
- 1½ tablespoons nam prik pao chili paste

Nam prik pao chili paste is available for sale outside of Thailand, such as the brand pictured here, but may be hard to find. To make your own, here's a simple recipe to make about 3 tablespoons:

- 2 tablespoons vegetable oil
- 1½ tablespoons soy sauce
- 1 tablespoon sugar
- 1 teaspoon miso (fermented soy bean paste)
- 1 teaspoon sour tamarind (substitute: 1 teaspoon lime juice)

- 1 teaspoon dried chili peppers
- 1 small shallot

Easy and quick!

Crush the dried chili peppers to flakes.

Heat, stirring constantly in a dry frying pan. Make sure you have good ventilation to do this!

Dry fry until the chilies start to darken to a deep reddish brown.

Add with all other ingredients in a blender or food processor and blend to a paste. Done!

Step 2: Veggie and Egg Preparation

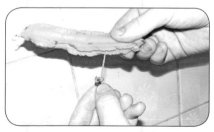

In this step, you'll need the egg and the winged beans (or other vegetables).

Put a small pot of water to boil.

Add an egg and boil it for 6–7 minutes.

Prepare your veggies.

If you're using winged beans, be sure to take off the ends and pull out the strings if your beans are mature (see photo).

Cut into small (1 cm) pieces.

Add them to the boiling water for the last few minutes (about 3 for winged beans) so they're cooked through.

Remove from heat, drain, and set aside.

Step 3: Fry Shallots (hawm jiow)

For this step you'll use the shallots and vegetable oil.

Peel the shallots (hawm) and slice them into nice rings.

An easy way to do this is to roll them on the cutting board, pressing down firmly with your hand, then slice off the top and bottom.

The peel comes away easily after that.

Heat the oil in a wok.

When it's really hot, toss in the shallots, then immediately turn the heat down to medium-low.

This shocks the outside of the shallots so they don't get too oily.

In Thai, *jiow* means to cook something by stirring it constantly in hot oil, and stirring is the key!

Make sure you don't stop stirring as the shallots on the border of the oil and wok edge will burn quickly and be gross.

Cook on medium-low heat for about 5 minutes until the shallots turn a nice light brown, then take out, drain, and set aside.

Be patient, Grasshopper, and you will be rewarded with an unrivaled aroma!

Step 4: Makin' the Sauce

This is where it gets crazy!

Well, maybe not crazy, but this is where the sauce is born which is, you know, pretty important.

You'll need everything else that hasn't been used yet.

First, crush the peanuts to a rough powder. This is best achieved using a mortar and pestle, but you could give them a quick pulse, or hide them in a folded over piece of wax paper and bash them with your shoe.

All on HIGH heat:

Next, heat up the oil left in the pan from the last step (unless you used it to make an omelette, which is highly recommended).

Smash the garlic clove and toss it in.

Stir for a few seconds, then pour in your coconut milk.

Add:

- sugar (about ⅔ tablespoon)
- soy sauce (several squirts)
- nam prik pao
- dried chili flakes and/or fresh, chopped chilies *
- vinegar (a few squirts)

*This dish is supposed to be moderately hot, with a great chili taste, so don't go overboard—you can always garnish with extra chilies for the maniacs you know and love!

Stir everything together to end up with a thick, orange-ish sauce. This should only take about 2 minutes.

Add in the crushed peanuts and take the sauce off the heat.

Squeeze the juice of half a lime on it and stir all-together.

Taste test!

Add sugar, soy sauce, or chilies if you think it needs more.

Always add a little in the beginning, then more at the end if it needs it so you don't go overboard!

When you're happy with your creation, turn the heat back on, stir the cooked beans into the sauce for 1 minute, then plate.

Almost done!

Step 5: Plate It, Serve It

Remember that hard boiled egg?

What about those fried shallots?

This is where their glory is achieved!

Pour the beans in sauce onto a big plate, and dress with crispy fried shallots, sliced egg, and colorful fresh chili peppers.

CONGRATULATIONS, YOU DID IT!

Eat this over rice with other fine dishes, such as a dill omelette!

IT TASTES GOOD!!!!!

Desserts

Coconut Whipped Cream

Creepy Coconut Kiwi Panna Cotta

Love Popsicles

Piña Colada Pie

100 Calorie Peanut Butter Chocolate Popsicles

Vegan Peach Basil Ice Cream

Chunky Chocolate Freezer Fudge (Dairy Free)

Chocolate Coconut Almond Ice Cream (Dairy Free)

Frog Egg Pudding

Layered Potato Dessert

Coconut Cream Pie

Chocolate Macaroon Soup with Almond Biscotti Croutons

Pumpkin Jello

Cassava Cake with Shredded Coconut

Easy Coconut Lime Avocado Cream

Sweet Potato Pie

(Pi)ña Colada

Malaysian Coconut Balls

Mochiko Cake with your Favorite Berries

Green Tea Mochi Cake

Coconut Whipped Cream

by annahowardshaw
www.instructables.com/id/
Coconut-Whipped-Cream/

Cutting down or eliminating dairy, but still want something to top pumpkin pie, crazy pancakes, or simply to dip strawberries in? Coconut milk makes just as thick and rich whipped cream as whipping cream, if not more! And the only difference in preparation is to remember to put the coconut milk in the fridge long enough to chill.

An additional plus is that whipped coconut cream does not break down the way dairy does. This whipped cream can be covered and stored for up to a few days without separation taking place. That alone makes it a better option in my book!

Step 1: Ingredients

- 1 can coconut milk (14 ounces)
- 2 tablespoons powdered sugar
- ½ teaspoon vanilla (optional)

Optional Ingredients:

- 1 teaspoons matcha
- 1 tablespoon cocoa powder
- 2 tablespoons pomegranate juice

Step 2: Directions

Set can of coconut milk and mixing bowl in the fridge overnight.

Set beaters in freezer for a few minutes before you begin.

Open can and remove all the solid coconut cream (leaving about ¼ can of coconut water).

Mix cream in chilled bowl with chilled beaters until fluffy (3 minutes or so).

Mix in powdered sugar and/or any other flavoring.

Use right away or cover and keep in the refrigerator for up to 3 days.

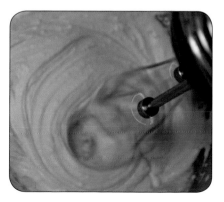

Creepy Coconut Kiwi Panna Cotta

by kitchentablescraps
www.instructables.com/id/
Creepy-Coconut-Kiwi-Panna-
Cotta/

I'm usually not one for gore. I hate scary movies (almost always). But if there was ever a time for a little gross-out fun it is late October. And I'm not such a scrooge that I can't enjoy a little Halloween silliness. So why not make a good dish, while you're at it? The elements of this dish are all natural: the white is a coconut panna cotta, the iris a cut fresh kiwi, the pupil is made of plumped raisins, and the blood is simply a raspberry coulis. The one element that is just for looks is the lens that sits on top of the kiwi iris (a little gelatin sheet). While it doesn't really add anything to the flavor of the dish, it makes the eye look

much more convincing. Plated in a different way, this dish could be a dessert for any night of the year.

Because you need the eyeball to hold its shape for this plating, I added a teensy bit more gelatin than I would normally put in a panna cotta. (I'd cut back by a ¼ tsp. if you're not doing the eyeball plating.) To make the panna cotta have a more delicate texture for serving, you can leave it out at room temperature for a half an hour before serving. Then plate it with hot raspberry coulis and the gelatin will soften just a bit. You can make this dessert a day in advance, but decrease the gelatin quantity by ⅛ tsp, as the gelatin will continue to firm up as the dessert sits refrigerated.

Step 1: Ingredients
Panna Cotta:
- ⅓ cup shredded, dried coconut (unsweetened)
- ¼ cup raisins or other dark-colored dried fruit.
- 1½ teaspoon unflavored, powdered gelatin
- 1 tablespoon rum (optional, substitute water if you prefer)
- 1 cup whole milk
- 1 cup coconut milk
- ¼ cup sugar
- 3 kiwis

Coulis:
- 1-2 cups frozen raspberries
- sugar

Lens:
- 1½ teaspoon gelatin
- ½ cup boiling water
- 1 tablespoon lime juice

- 1 tablespoon sugar
  Yield: 6 servings

Equipment:

- ½ cup mise en place bowls or half-sphere molds
- melon baller
- 1½" circle cutter

Step 2: Infuse Cream

Place coconut flakes on a baking sheet, and toast in a 350° F oven for 3–6 minutes until lightly browned. Keep an eye on the coconut and stir it at least once mid cooking. (It cooks more quickly at the edges of the pan.) Place raisins in a jar and cover with warm water.

Infuse coconut cream

Measure gelatin into a small bowl and stir in the rum or water. Leave it to sit for a few minutes. Place the milk, coconut milk, coconut flakes, and sugar in a saucepan over high heat. Stir the pan frequently as the cream is heating to prevent scorching. Watch carefully as the mixture will boil over very quickly. Once the mixture has just come to a boil, remove the pan from the heat, cover, and let sit for at least 15 minutes.

Step 3: Cut Kiwis

Skin kiwis and cut the end of the kiwi off. You want to cut enough off the end to have a 1½" circle for the iris of your eye. Place the end of a kiwi into your mise en place bowl or mold and carefully mark the side of the kiwi with a knife. Cut the kiwi so that it will be exactly the height of the mold. Use your circle cutter to cut the kiwi into a perfect cylinder. (If you don't have a circle cutter, you can just carefully trim the kiwi into a circle.) Last, use a melon baller to scoop out a half sphere where you want the pupil to be. Put the little half sphere back into the kiwi for the moment. Spray your molds with non-stick cooking spray. Invert the kiwi half (so the scooped-out side is facing down) and place in the center of your mold. Repeat with the other kiwis until you have filled up all your molds.

Step 4: Mold

By now, your coconut milk mixture should have an incredible coconut aroma and flavor. Strain the coconut flakes out of the mixture and pour it back into your saucepan. Add the gelatin/rum mixture to the saucepan and place over medium high heat. Stir constantly until the mixture is steaming, and all of the gelatin has dissolved. Strain the mixture into a liquid measuring cup. Pour your panna cotta into the molds. Fill them as close to completely full as you can. Carefully move the molds to the refrigerator. Refrigerate for 3-4 hours, until set.

Step 5: Make Lenses

Stir together gelatin, lime juice and sugar. Pour boiling water over the mix and stir until all of the gelatin granules are dissolved. Pour gelatin into muffin-tin liners. (Make a few more lenses than you plan to use, just in case you tear one accidentally.) Refrigerate the muffin cups until the gelatin has set (check in about half an hour). Once the gelatin is quite firm, carefully peel back the muffin tin liners and remove the gelatin layer. If you are having trouble releasing them, you can dip them in hot water for a second or two. The heat will melt the gelatin at the edges and release the rest of the mold. Use your circle cutter to

cut the lenses into perfect circles, the same size as your kiwi iris.

Boil a few cups of water. Pour the hot water into a bowl and, one at a time, dip your panna cotta molds for 3–4 seconds. Carefully press around the edge of the mold with a moistened finger to release the edges of the panna cotta. Place a plate on top of the mold and invert both the plate and the mold. Slowly lift up the mold, peeking to make sure that the panna cotta is releasing onto the plate. Pop out the half-sphere of kiwi, and clean up any bits of panna cotta on top of the kiwi. Drain your raisins and press a few raisins into your melon baller to make a half-sphere of raisins. Place the raisin pupil in the kiwi cavity. Finally, place the lens over the kiwi iris. The edge of the lens will look a little harsh. To sculpt it into a more natural looking rounded lens, dip a paring knife into very hot water, and hold the hot knife against the edge of the lens. You don't need to cut the edge away, just use the hot knife to melt it.

For the coulis, heat raspberries in a saucepan. Stir to break up the fruit. Sweeten to taste and strain. Pour warm coulis around the edge of the panna cottas. Go ahead, add a few spatters for flair, too.

Enjoy, and have a very happy Halloween!

These are coconut-strawberry popsicles, made using a paletas recipe. Paletas are Mexican popsicles made with fresh fruit. I came up with the idea for these popsicles when brainstorming for the Instructables Frozen Treats Contest. I was inspired by previous photos I'd seen of popsicles made with whole pieces of fruit. I thought they looked just beautiful and wanted to attempt the same.

Step 1: Ingredients

- 14 oz can of coconut milk
- ½ cup sugar
- ½ cup heavy cream
- ½ cup milk
- ¼ teaspoon vanilla sweetened coconut flakes
- 1 cup ice cubes
- popsicle mold w/sticks

    * This recipe makes about 8 popsicles

The popsicle molds were a bit tricky to find now that it's the end of summer, but I did manage to find a set of 4 at Target.

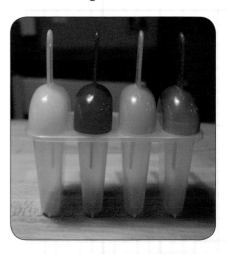

Step 2: Make the Popsicles

On the stove, bring the coconut milk to a slow simmer. Add the sugar and stir occasionally until the sugar has melted into the milk. Remove from the heat and pour it into a large bowl, preferably one that will be easy to pour from later. Add some ice to cool the coconut milk. When the ice is melted, add in the milk, heavy cream, vanilla, and coconut flakes. I started with adding about ½ cup of coconut flakes but kept adding more until I might have added about a cup. I felt that it was enough when I gave it a stir and it was clear that there were coconut flakes.

Pour the coconut mixture into each mold until about ¾ full. Set aside and now you're ready to prepare the strawberries.

Step 3: Making Strawberry Hearts

I had fun with this step and I think that you'll find that it turns out to be easier then you'd think.

After selecting the strawberries that you think are the best, de-stem them and slice them in half. Once they're in half, you'll notice that some are slightly hollow on the inside. Choose those that aren't, it'll make positioning them within the popsicle mold easier and give you better clarity of color.

Turn the half-strawberry slice on its side and cut a thin slice. Make a few slices until the half is cut up. Try to make the slices as straight as possible so that the strawberry slivers are flat.

Now you can probably begin to see the outline of hearts in the slices of strawberry that you've made. Using a knife, trim the tops of each slice so that the arches are more pronounced. Make many of them so that you have a selection of the best ones. I found myself not choosing the ones that were very white in the center. Snack away on those that don't work quite right!

Step 4: Assembly

Putting it all together!

Now that the strawberry pieces are prepared, you are ready to place them in the popsicle molds. Place a strawberry slice at the top of a mold with the arches of the heart pointing downwards. Using a utensil, press the strawberry slice as flat to the side of the mold as possible and slide it down into the mold. In general, I found that the strawberry slices would stick rather well to the side of the mold. If one does start to float or isn't sticking very well, then pull it out and pick a different slice from the selection. I chose a knife to help me in positioning the strawberries. You can place strawberry hearts on both sides of the popsicle mold.

After you are happy with how it looks, add more of the coconut mixture until the popsicle mold is almost full. To top it off, I added some more small slices of strawberries. These can be leftovers from making the heart shapes. I did this at first as an attempt to keep the strawberries from floating to the top while the molds were in the freezer. I found that this did help and also was a delicious addition. I really like the combination of the coconut and strawberry flavors. With just the heart shape made out of strawberry, adding more to the bottom of the popsicle helped to balance the flavors more.

Once you are finished, add the top to the popsicle mold and place them in the freezer.

Step 5: Enjoy!

After the popsicles are frozen (a few hours or more), remove them from the freezer. I ran mine under hot water for a few seconds to loosen them up in the molds.

And enjoy!

This is an instructable for a Piña Colada pie I invented. I looked it up and saw one recipe similar to mine, but I think mine tastes better. Hope you enjoy my recipe.

Step 1: Ingredients

Here are all the things you will need to make your pie:

For the crust:
- ⅓ cup plus one tablespoon of shortening (or ⅓ cup of lard)
- 1 cup of all purpose flour
- ½ teaspoon of salt
- 2–3 tablespoons of cold water

For the filling:
- ¾ cup sugar
- ½ teaspoon salt
- 3 tablespoons cornstarch
- 1½ cup coconut milk
- 1½ cup milk
- 3 eggs
- 3 tablespoons butter
- ¾ teaspoon vanilla
- ½ cup coconut flakes

For the topping:
- whipped cream
- 1 jar of Maraschino cherries
- 2 tablespoon coconut flakes
  Other: 1 can pineapple

Step 2: The Piecrust

The first step is the piecrust.

Take your flour and salt and mix them in a medium-sized bowl.

Then put your shortening (or lard) in the bowl and cut it into the flour and salt using a pastry blender. Do this until the particles are the size of peas.

Next, slowly mix your water into the dough until it pulls away from the side of the bowl.

Sprinkle some flour on a clean surface and your hands and roll out your dough. Remember, short, quick rolls away from the center, moving around in a circle. Never roll back and forth.

Place your dough in your pan and even it out, making sure it overhangs the edge of the pan a bit.

Crinkle your edges. To do this place two fingers on one side of the dough at the top and push with your thumb to force the dough in between your fingers, then pinch. (see picture)

Finally, take your crust and put it in the freezer for later.

Step 3: The Filling

Now it's time to make the filling.

Spread 1 cup pineapple chunks on the piecrust.

Place coconut in heavy bottom skillet and toast over low heat, until golden brown.

In a heavy saucepan combine sugar, cornstarch, and salt.

Stir in milk and coconut milk.

Cook and stir over medium heat until thick and bubbly. Cook and stir 2 minutes more. Remove from heat and gradually stir in 1 cup of the hot mixture into egg yolks.

Pour egg mixture back into pan, stirring with a whisk.

Cook and stir 2 minutes more.

Remove from heat and stir in butter and vanilla, until butter melts. Add coconut, and stir until combined and pour into pie shell.

Set the pie aside to cool.

Step 4: The Pie Topping

When the pie has cooled mix together your topping.

For the topping on the pie simply mix whipped cream with the juice from the marischino cherries and pour onto cold pie.

Then toast enough coconut to your taste and sprinkle on top of pie. Place your pie in the fridge for 1–2 hours.

Step 5: Enjoy!

Now simply cut yourself a piece and enjoy!

100 Calorie Peanut Butter Chocolate Popsicles

by rvt1985

www.instructables.com/id/
100-Calorie-Peanut-Butter-
Chocolate-Popsicles/

These tasty popsicles feature PB2, chocolate and plain flavors, and vanilla flavored coconut milk. Satisfy your sweet tooth for 100 calories, and get 5 grams of protein as well.

Step 1: Gather Ingredients and Tools

Ingredients:

1 Chocolate Popsicle:
- 2 tablespoons chocolate PB2
- ¼ cup vanilla coconut milk
- 1 small cookies and cream bar

1 peanut butter popsicle:
- 2 tablespoons of regular PB2
- ¼ cup of vanilla coconut milk
- ½ tablespoon of cacao nibs (sweetened or unsweetened)

Tools:
- knife and cutting board/plate
- popsicle molds or Dixie cups
- popsicle sticks
- bowl and spoon
- 1 tablespoon

Step 2: Mix it Up!

Shake the coconut milk well and use a spoon to stir in the PB2. After the liquid is smooth, add the chopped candy or cacao nibs

Made following the recipes above, here's the nutritional info:

Chocolate, Cookies, and Cream bar:

133.5 Calories (if you use the whole small candy bar, I did not) / 5.5 grams of fat / 5 grams of protein

Peanut butter and Cacao nibs:

100 calories / 5.5 grams of fat / 5 grams of protein

Feel free to make the mixture richer by adding an extra tablespoon of PB2 and reducing the coconut milk. You can also mix and match with candy and cacao nibs or leave them out all together.

Amazon.com has a great price on a 2 pack of PB2.

Step 3: Pour into Molds

Pour the mixture into the molds. For extra fanciness, add a few cacao nibs or candy pieces to the base of the popsicle. Freeze for a minimum of 4 hours. These molds were tricky to remove the popsicles from, but perhaps paper Dixie cups would work better.

Step 4: Eat Up!

Remove from the molds with the help of a butter knife, if needed. Enjoy your not-so-hard work!

Vegan Peach Basil Ice Cream

by kerri2357

www.instructables.com/id/
Vegan-Peach-Basil-Ice-
Cream/

- Blender
- Ice cream freezer

Who doesn't love a frozen dessert on a sultry evening? This vegan ice cream is delicious and couldn't be easier to make.

Step 1: Here's What You Need

- 2 14-oz cans of coconut milk (I used lower fat and got a texture more like ice milk. Use the full-fat versions to get a richer finished product.)
- ¾ cup of sugar
- one bunch of basil
- 1 cup of peaches (about 4 halves, if using jarred)
- 1 teaspoon vanilla

Step 2: Getting Started

Put coconut milk and sugar in the blender and blend for 30 seconds.

Add peaches and vanilla, pulse to break up the peaches. Bruise the basil by whacking it with the back of a knife and put that in the blender to steep.

Place in the fridge to steep for at least 30 minutes, or up to a few hours before you're ready to put it into the machine.

Step 3: Freeze!

Remove it from the fridge, remove basil, and taste. The basil taste will be subtle, but if you want a stronger flavor (like I did) tear several leaves and put them back in before you put the mixture into the ice cream freezer.

Freeze mixture according to the machine's directions. When you have soft frozen ice cream, transfer to small containers to freeze to desired firmness. I used small cardboard loaf pans lined with plastic wrap.

Step 4: Yum!

Once it's frozen to the consistency you like, scoop it out and enjoy!

This would also be good with strawberry and mint, or mango and basil or mint. If you make a variation and like it, share it in the comments below. Thanks!

Chunky Chocolate Freezer Fudge (Dairy Free)

by savynaturalista
www.instructables.com/id/
Chunky-Chocolate-Freezer-
Fudge-Dairy-Free/

Ingredients:

- 3¾ cups dairy free chocolate chips (I used carob)
- 1 can coconut milk
- ¼ cup butter substitute (I used earth balance)
- 1 cup nuts (optional)

Recipe Directions:

Place saran wrap in an 8 × 8 baking dish and set aside. In a microwave safe bowl place chocolate chips, coconut milk, and butter; microwave for 3–5 minutes stirring chocolate until it has melted completely. Once the chocolate has completely melted, slowly stir in nuts and place in baking dish. Once done place in freezer until the fudge sets. Cut into pieces and serve.

Chocolate Coconut Almond Ice Cream (Dairy Free)

by Henrie Marie
www.instructables.com/id/
Homemade-Almond-Joy-Ice-
Cream-dairy-free-1/

Homemade Chocolate Coconut Almond Ice Cream—dairy free, vegan, gluten free, cholesterol free, ice cream maker free.

This recipe came out amazing. Frozen version of one of your favorite candy bars. The ice cream is creamy and loaded with coconut so it has that dense coconut texture just like the candy bar and the chocolate hardens once it hits the cold ice cream to form a chocolate shell.

Here is what you will need to make this yummy cold treat in your own kitchen, without an ice cream maker.

Ingredients—for two cups of ice cream
- 1¼ cup of almond and coconut blended milk
- ½ can of sweetened cream of coconut (can be found in the cocktail mixer section of your grocery store)
- ½ cup shredded coconut
- ¼ cup sugar in the raw (unrefined sugar or vegan sugar)
- 2 tablespoons corn starch
- slivered or whole plain almonds

Chocolate Sauce:
- ½ cup dark chocolate chips
- 1 tablespoon coconut oil

Directions:

Mix two tablespoons of corn starch with ¼ cup of almond/coconut blend milk. Set aside.

On medium/high heat combine one cup of almond/coconut blend milk and ¼ cup sugar. Bring to a boil. This will be ample time for the sugar to melt. Remove from heat and add the corn starch to the almond/coconut milk mixture. Let cool completely.

In a mixing bowl or with a hand held mixer whip half a can of cream of coconut until its white and forms stiff peaks.

Add the cooled almond/coconut mixture to the whipped cream of coconut and mix well. Incorporate the shredded coconut flakes into the mixture and transfer to a freezer safe container. Freeze overnight.

Chocolate sauce: In a double boiler, melt the chocolate chips and coconut oil until silky smooth. Keep at room temperature so it does not harden. It will harden once it comes into contact with cold temperatures.

Top the ice cream with almonds and ENJOY!

chunky chocolate freezer fudge (dairy free)

CALLING ALL BIOLOGY TEACHERS!!! If you are looking for a fun snack to go along with your amphibians chapter this year, then look no further. This recipe is a playful spin on tapioca pudding. There are two things that have always reminded me of frog eggs; one is tapioca pudding and the other is kiwis.. So I decided to combine the two and create a desert that has the appearance and texture of frog eggs!

Ingredients:
- 3 tablespoons instant tapioca
- 2 cups of milk
- ¾ cup of coconut milk
- 6 tablespoons of sugar (you can reduce this if you would like. The coconut milk is fairly sweet on its own)
- 1 egg lightly beaten
- 2 kiwis
- green food coloring

   OPTIONAL: 1 teaspoon vanilla (the recipe on the box calls for vanilla but I made mine without and it was great)

Recipe:
   In a microwavable bowl, mix together the tapioca, milk, coconut milk, sugar, and the egg.

Let it sit for 5 minutes.

Cook it in the microwave on high for 12 minutes (stopping to stir it every 3 minutes). While it's cooking peel and mash the kiwis with a fork.

Once it's cooked remove it and stir in the kiwis and a few drops of green food coloring. (Add your vanilla if you would like.) Refrigerate for 20 minutes to cool.

NOW YOU CAN EAT IT!

Serve:
   I spooned it into glasses and topped it off with some whipped cream and a plastic frog. My children loved it! They were all smiles and giggles! I think the flavors together are delicious too. The coconut compliments the tartness of the kiwi perfectly.

HAPPY CREATING!

Layered Potato Dessert

by cupritte
www.instructables.com/id/
Layered-Potato-Dessert/

I grew up in Hawaii, and there are these great potatoes that are common to find in markets called Okinawan Sweet Potatoes. They are tan on the outside and purple on the inside. When prepared they have a custardy texture and are quite sweet. I recently re-discovered these when making baby food. I found that they taste amazing with bananas and was determined to make an adult dessert with this idea.

This dessert has a lot of possibilities. I realized this morning that it would be easy to do a version of this with no refined sugar, or a vegan version. The one I did today has a little sugar added and a little milk but those could easily be excluded depending on the needs of the chef.

The dessert I made today has four layers to it.

Step 1: Ingredients
Almond Gelatin Dessert
- pre-mixed packet of Almond Flavor Gelatin Dessert which you can find at Asian grocers
- 2 cups milk (you can use any type of milk you like, it's pretty flexible. You could even use water.)

Puréed Sweet Potato
- 2 Okinawan sweet potatoes (tan exterior, purple interior) or other type of sweet potato (I used local purple sweet potatoes) baked or steamed
- water or milk to blend

Banana
- 2–3 or more bananas

Coconut Whipped Cream
- can of coconut milk
- 1 teaspoon powdered sugar (optional)

If you are thinking about doing this recipe go ahead and get a can of coconut milk and stick it in your fridge now. It takes a day to set up, and as long as you've got the space, you might as well put one in, and then it will be ready once you get the rest of the ingredients and motivation to make the recipe.

Step 2: Prep and Purée the Potatoes

One of the nice things about this dessert is you can do it all ahead of time at whatever speed you want.

Here's the quick version:

Put the coconut milk in the fridge!

Peel and steam/boil potatoes or bake them.

Then purée in the blender, add potato water, milk, and sugar as necessary for taste and blending a smooth pudding like texture.

Here is the long one:

As I mentioned before the first step is putting the coconut milk in the fridge. I didn't realize it needed a day to set up and a few days ago was like, "Oh I'll make dessert today." No dice. Don't be like me. Stick it in now. It needs time to cool and separate milk and coconut water.

Next is to prep your potatoes. If you get Okinawan sweet potatoes, they are fairly soft on the inside (about the consistency of a normal orange sweet potato) so you can peel them and cut them up and steam or boil them in a little water. I

like this preparation for the potatoes because it makes them nice and soft and you have the extra potato flavored water to add to your purée.

So like I said, peel the skin. Take out any icky bits, like the potato eyes or anything else you don't want in your purée and then chop and steam or boil. It takes about half an hour to get them soft, depending on how big your pieces are. If they are smaller check them at 20 minutes, and once they are soft take them off the heat to cool.

Now as I mentioned I didn't have Okinawan sweet potatoes for this batch, so I went with local purple sweet potatoes. Now these things are far more dense and quite annoying (and even scary) to chop into cubes when raw. So I washed them, and then baked them at 375 degrees for about 40 minutes. Actually I think I baked them a little longer, then just turned off the oven and let them cool inside, as they were a little dry, but whatever. Bake them. After that . . . I threw mine in the fridge for two days because I had to make baby food. Potatoes are forgiving.

Eventually blend them. If I had steamed them I would have added the potatoes and the some of the potato water to the blender once they had cooled until I got a nice smooth but thick consistency. As I mentioned my baked potatoes were kind of dry so I added some milk and then some yogurt. I also added a bit of sugar. If I had been making this for company I would have added more sugar. If you are using Okinawan Sweet Potatoes you probably won't need it. In mine it barely made a difference so I either needed to add more or just skip the sugar altogether.

By the way, I'm sure most of us have had the experience of spilling something because of taking a picture at the same time right?

Step 2: Make Gelatin Dessert

I like these pre mixed packets of Almond Dessert so that's what I used. You could easily go with something sugar free or a different flavor or even make your own with a bit of agar (assuming your vegan) or gelatin or skip it all together. (It wouldn't really be missing much.)

These take two hours to set so while your potatoes are cooling get your gelatin going. I just followed the instructions on the back of the box. Mix contents with 4 cups water in a saucepan, bring to a boil stirring occasionally. Remove from heat.

Stir in 2 cups whole milk (I used 1%, it's flexible and really doesn't matter)

Pour mixture into glasses or shallow pan and let cool. (I used a casserole pan, I like to cut shapes out of it.)

Refrigerate until set, about 2 hours.

Done!

Step 3: Coconut Whip

Now for the coconut topping.

I have an iSi whipped cream tool (toy) so I used that to make my whipped cream.

If you don't have one of these spiffy toys there is a fantastic instructable on how to make the coconut whipped cream!

I took the thick cream from the top of the can in the fridge and scraped it into my whipped cream maker. I left the majority of the water in the can, and as I had kind of jostled the can there was a good amount of cream in the can, and I poured off the water to get the rest. I added about ½ teaspoon (a pinch) of confectioners' sugar to the cream then charged my canister. I thought the coconut cream would need the confectioners' sugar to stabilize but with the whipper I don't think it did. The cream came out nice and thick and was very stable (holding up better than normal whipped cream, but then my coconut cream was really thick). I think as long as you don't add a ton of the coconut water to it, the whipped cream should be fairly forgiving.

Step 4: Put It All Together

When I originally had this idea, I thought it would be cool to serve it like a parfait. But that was before I added the coconut jell to the mix. So I tried that and a little more formal type of display for the desserts.

For the parfait I made small rectangles out of the gelatin and put those in the bottom, then a layer of the potato, then some sliced banana and the coconut cream to top. This would work great to feed a larger group in a big dish. The other method I used was I took a cookie cutter and cut a slice of the gelatin and layered the potato and cream on top and it looked best when surrounded by the banana rather than layering it in. Plus the gelatin slides on the plate very easily and the bananas slow that down a bit.

In either case, the potato and the coconut whipped cream have potential to be quite rich, so try them first, and then decide what ratio you would like to use. Mine was a bit heavy on both, Next time I would use a smaller layer of the potato and cream. I also might add in a little more of the coconut water to the whipper as the cream was quite heavy.

I hope that you enjoyed the recipe and have lots of fun doing your own cooking experiments with it!

Coconut Cream Pie

by canida
www.instructables.com/id/
Coconut-Cream-Pie/

This pie is a bit on the subtle side of things. If you want a stronger coconut flavor, swap about half of the vanilla extract listed below for coconut extract. You can also swap in more coconut butter in place of normal butter, and use coconut rum in place of the vodka. I unfortunately didn't have any coconut extract on hand, so if you try this let me know how it goes!

Step 1: Crust Ingredients
- 1⅓ cups flour
- 1 tablespoon sugar
- ½ teaspoon salt
- 1 stick (½ cup) cold butter, chunked
- 3–4 Tablespoons cold vodka

Filling Ingredients:
- 1 can (2 cups) coconut milk
- ⅔ cup sugar

- 4 large egg yolks
- 3 tablespoons flour
- 2 tablespoons cornstarch
- pinch salt
- 3 tablespoons coconut butter
- ¾ cup finely shredded unsweetened coconut
- ½ teaspoon vanilla extract

Topping Ingredients:
- 1 cup whipping cream
- 2 tablespoons powdered sugar
- ¼ teaspoon vanilla
- 2–3 tablespoons toasted coconut (I used a mix of fine and coarsely shredded coconut)

Tools:
- bowl
- rubber/silicone spatula
- food processor, pastry blender, or two knives
- rolling pin or cylindrical bottle
- pie plate
- aluminum foil
- pie weights (coins, rice, beans, etc)
- heavy-bottomed pot
- whisk
- electric mixer (hand or stand) unless you're crazy good with that whisk

Step 2: Make Crust
Combine flour, salt, sugar.

Add cold butter, and pulse in food processor (or cut in with pastry blender or two knives).

Continue until mix is like coarse, pebbly sand.

Sprinkle with 1 tablespoon vodka, and pulse/mix again.

Add more vodka until dough sticks together when you pinch or roll a small ball.

Form into a disc and refrigerate until chilled (30 plus minutes).

Roll crust out, and transfer to your pie plate.

Line piecrust with foil.

Fill foil with pie weights (I use coins, beans, or rice).

Bake at 425° F for 12 minutes, then remove foil and bake for 10 more minutes.

Remove and cool completely.

Step 3: Make Filling

Heat coconut milk in microwave until lukewarm (remove from can first! Pyrex measuring cups are your friend).

Heat sugar and eggs until 2-3x fluffier, very thick, and pale yellow.

Slowly beat in flour, cornstarch, and salt. Scrape sides of bowl as needed.

Slowly beat in coconut milk, and beat until thoroughly mixed.

Pour into heavy-bottomed pan, and cook over medium-high heat, stirring constantly to prevent the mix from burning or separating—a whisk is best. (Really this isn't hard, and doesn't take too long—you just have to pay it full attention.)

Bring it to a boil for just a minute, then turn off the heat and keep stirring as it thickens.

Stir in coconut butter until it's thoroughly melted.

Add coconut and vanilla.

Transfer to a bowl (metal for fastest heat transfer) and chill until thoroughly set, at least 2 hours.

Step 4: Make Topping

Whip cream and powdered sugar until it forms stiff peaks.

Mix in vanilla.

Step 5: Assemble and Serve

Scoop about ¼ of the topping out and add it into the filling, gently stirring to incorporate.

Scoop filling into the piecrust, and smooth the top.

Scoop remaining topping on top, and shape it attractively.

Chill at least 30 minutes (so it sets properly) and up to 5 hours (crust starts to get soggy).

Sprinkle with toasted coconut just before serving.

Cut into wedges and eat.

Yum, delicious coconut pie!—if you have leftovers, cover with plastic wrap to prevent the pie from drying out.

Chocolate Macaroon Soup with Almond Biscotti Croutons

by annahowardshaw
www.instructables.com/id/
Chocolate-Macaroon-Soup-
with-Almond-Biscotti-Crout/

(Vegan) dessert soups are more often fruity, summer types dishes, but I wanted to make one that would be more appropriate for an insanely cold and dark February evening. Fair warning, this is super-rich, but if you like chocolate and coconut, this is basically a bowl of warm, melty macaroons. So, you'll probably dig it.

The biscotti adds texture and provides a less sweet counter taste (there is not as much sugar in this as most biscotti recipes) but I added a few other garnish suggestions as well.

Quick comment on egg replacer vs. cornstarch. I used both in this, but either one would do the trick. But I have found that in soups/sauces I can taste the egg replacer while cornstarch is not detectable.

Also, you'll notice I used date sugar. I'm sure regular sugar will work just fine, I'm just being a hippie about it.

Enjoy!

Step 1: Ingredients
Chocolate Soup
- 1 can coconut milk (14 ounces)
- ¼ cup date sugar
- 2 tablespoons raw cocoa powder
- 2 teaspoons amaretto
- 1 teaspoon vanilla
- 1 teaspoon corn starch

Biscotti Croutons
- 1 cup flour
- ¼ cup chopped almonds (or cocoa almonds)
- ⅛ cup date sugar
- 2 egg equivalent of egg replacer (I used Ener-G Egg Replacer)
- 1 teaspoon lemon zest
- 2 teaspoons amaretto
- 1 teaspoon chocolate extract
- ½ teaspoon baking powder
- ½ teaspoon baking soda
- ⅛ teaspoon salt
- ⅛ teaspoon cinnamon

Tools:
- Mixing bowls
- Baking Sheet
- Saucepan
- Whisk
- Serrated knife
- Chopping knife
- Cutting board

- Parchment paper
- Zester
- Measuring cups
- Measuring spoons
- Ramekins for serving
  Makes just over 2 servings.

Step 2: Make Biscotti

Preheat oven to 350° F.

Prepare egg replacer (1 Tbs egg replacer to 4 tablespoons water).

Chop almonds.

In a mixing bowl, combine flour, baking soda, baking powder, and salt.

In a separate bowl, mix egg replacer, amaretto, chocolate extract, lemon zest, and sugar.

Add flour to wet ingredients and mix by hand (dough will be dry, but should be able to stick together when pressed).

Mix in chopped almonds.

Form dough into a log and bake in oven for 20–25 minutes.

Step 3: Biscotti Continued

As the biscotti nears completion, I would suggest making the soup after Step 2 below.

Remove biscotti from oven (turn oven down to warm) and let them cool to the touch.

Using a serrated knife, cut into ½ inch pieces, lay on side, and return to the oven for 15 minutes to toast.

Once cooled, break into smaller pieces. Since this is the smallest biscotti recipe I thought would be reasonable to make, there will probably be more croutons than you want for the soup, so you might want to leave a few larger pieces to serve along with the dish or for coffee the next day.

And in case you don't want to spend this much time on what is basically a handful of crumbs, here are a few vegan and non-vegan alternative garnish suggestions . . .

- Chopped almonds and/or toasted coconut
- Whipped cream sprinkled with cocoa powder (there are vegan whipped cream recipes out there)
- Whipped cream with a cherry (that just goes well on most things)

- Marshmallows—hey, why not?

Add amaretto and vanilla.

Add cocoa powder and mix until smooth.

Pour into ramekins, top with biscotti croutons, and you're done.

Thanks for checking this out!

Step 4: Chocolate Soup

And now for the soup . . .

Prepare cornstarch (1 tsp cornstarch to 1 teaspoon water, mix until smooth)

Heat coconut milk in the saucepan and bring to a simmer, whisking occasionally (Note: Whisk pretty much continuously during all steps).

Add cornstarch.

Add date sugar and whisk until dissolved.

Pumpkin Jello
by canida
www.instructables.com/id/
Pumpkin-Jello/

I wanted pumpkin jello, but all I could find were complicated mousses and crustless pies. So I smooshed up one of the mousse recipes (minus the eggs and such) with a high-gelatin finger jello recipe and came up with a pumpkin jello that fit the bill perfectly.

I swapped the dairy for coconut milk, both to separate the flavor from a standard pumpkin pie and because it takes allspice (my favorite spice) quite nicely. And we still had Rachel's stash of coconut rum sitting around the lab, and I wanted to help use it up. The end result was awesome, delicious, and flexible.

Try it for Halloween, Thanksgiving, or any fall event—it's great finger food, so perfect for hors d'oeuvres. Yum. Bonus: it's gluten free (unlike all those pies) and you can make it vegan by subbing agar for the gelatin. Enjoy!

Step 1: Tools and Ingredients

For the pumpkin jello:

- 1 can pumpkin purée
- 1 can coconut milk
- 1 cup brown sugar
- 4 packets unflavored gelatin
- ½ cup flavored liquor(s) of your choice, or apple cider if you want to skip the alcohol
- ⅛ teaspoon salt
- ¼ teaspoon allspice
- ⅛ teaspoon cloves

For the whipped cream:

- 1 pint heavy whipping cream
- ¼ cup powdered sugar
- ⅛ tsp nutmeg (fresh grated is best)
- ⅛ tsp allspice or to taste
- 1 Tablespoon coconut rum (optional)

Tools:

- Electric mixer, or a whisk and stout arm
- 8 × 8 Pyrex pan, or a pie plate
- rubber spatula
- plastic bag cake decorating tips (optional)
- microwave

Add a roughly equal amount of the coconut milk.

Sprinkle gelatin over the top in a thin layer, and wait a minute or two while it slowly absorbs moisture from the liquid in the bowl, or "blooms." (This is necessary to prevent the gelatin from clumping.) Then stir the liquid to turn over the surface, and repeat until you've used all 4 packages. I found it best to do this about ½ a packet at a time.

If all the liquid has been absorbed (you see the surface buckling/getting bumpy), pour in more coconut milk and keep going.

Check out the picture—you can see yellowish surfaces (gelatin that has absorbed moisture), white powder (gelatin that's still dry), and some crenelation (areas where there's not enough moisture available—I should have added more liquid).

Step 2: Bloom Gelatin

Pour the ½ cup booze (or apple cider) into a wide, flat bowl.

Step 3: Prep Pumpkin

Dump pumpkin purée in a microwave-safe bowl, along with

the rest of the coconut milk. Whisk together, then microwave until the mixture is warm but not hot/cooked. (You should be able to stick your finger in the mix, but won't want to leave it there.)

The time will vary with bowl type and microwave strength. I recommend microwaving in one-minute increments, then stirring and doing the finger test between.

Step 4: Combine and Chill

Scoop your nicely bloomed gelatin into the warm pumpkin/coconut milk mixture (or the other way around—it doesn't really matter) and whisk together. The heat should help dissolve any residual clumps in the gelatin mix, but if you see any be sure to whisk a bit longer.

Add 1 cup brown sugar, ⅛ teaspoon salt, ¼ teaspoon allspice, and ⅛ teaspoon cloves. Whisk again until everything is mixed.

Pour the jello mixture into an 8 × 8 Pyrex pan, or a deep-dish pie pan, and put in the fridge for several hours or overnight.

Step 5: Whip Cream

1 pint heavy whipping cream (this is called different things in different countries—use whatever you'd normally use for whipped cream)

Dump your pint of chilled whipping cream into a bowl, and whip. The Instructables lab has a snazzy robot-themed Kitchenaid mixer, but you'll do fine with hand-held beaters or a whisk and some well-developed whisking muscles. Go to town.

As the cream reaches soft peaks, add the powdered sugar, rum, and spices. Continue whipping until the cream is light and fluffy and keeps its shape well when you sneak a scoop with your (clean) finger.

Chill until ready to serve, up to one day.

Step 6: Remove and Cut Jello

Remove your jello pan from the fridge, and poke it in the center to be sure it's properly set up. If all's well, the center and the edges should feel equally firm.

Removing the jello:

Grab a knife or rubber spatula, and work it around the edge of your pan to separate the edges from the pan. Identify a cutting board large enough to accommodate the jello pan, and place it strategically near the sink.

Next, fill your sink with hot tap water, and gently lower the pan into the water, being sure to hold on to the handles. You don't want to set the pan down—the hot water should be performing its melty magic on the bottom surface of the pan. Count slowly to 10.

Now, put the pan on the counter, and place the cutting board on top of it. Hold the pan and cutting board together, and flip them over. The heat will have mostly detached the jello from the pan, so wiggle or tap it gently to break the seal and let the jello slide out.

Slice the jello into shapes of your choice with a sharp knife (rinse in hot water between cuts to make them super-clean) or use cookie cutters. Put your jello shapes on a plate, and return them to the fridge until almost ready to serve.

Step 7: Decorate and Serve

Place a dollop of whipped cream on top of each piece of pumpkin jello. If you want to get fancy, use a baggie and a cake decorating tip to squeeze a large rosette of whipped cream into place. Use some of the less-pretty side/corner pieces to test the proper jello-to-whipped cream ratio; I come down on the "tons of whipped cream" side so added more to the ones you see here when I ate them.

You can store the topped jello pieces in the fridge, though they'll last for hours in a room so long as it's not too hot. Ours all disappeared quickly!

Cassava Cake with Shredded Coconut

by rmedan
www.instructables.com/id/
Cassava-Cake-with-
Shredded-Coconut/

Ingredients:
- 3.5 oz (100g) shredded coconut
- ⅛ teaspoons of salt
- 14 oz (400g) grated cassava (tapioca)
- 3½ oz (100g) sugar
- 4½ oz (125g) coconut milk
- 2 oz (50g) water
- 2 tablespoons potato starch
- Pinch of salt
- 3–4 screwpine (pandan) leaves, cut into 4–5" (10-12cm) lengths
- 1 banana leaf (optional)
- Water, for boiling

Serves 4 | Prep Time: 10 minutes | Cook Time: 40 minutes

Method:
Heat up the water in a wok/pot big enough for a 6.5" square pan.

Combine the shredded coconut with ⅛ teaspoon salt in a stainless steel dish and steam for 3–4 minutes. Set aside to cool.

Use a food processor to mix the grated cassava, sugar, coconut milk, water, potato starch, and pinch of salt until well mixed, about 30–45 seconds.

Pour the mixture into a 6.5" (17cm) square pan. Level the top of the mixture with the base of a spoon. Layer the screwpine leaves flat on top of the mixture. Steam the cassava mixture for 35–40 minutes on medium heat.

Remove the pan from the streaming tray when it is done. Let it cool completely before cutting. Cut into small squares and toss with the shredded coconut before serving.

Serve steamed Cassava with Shredded Coconut on the banana leaf (optional).

Cook's Notes:
You can use frozen grated cassava if you can't find fresh cassava. If using frozen cassava, squeeze out the liquid from the defrosted grated cassava before use. This recipe calls for fresh shredded coconut or frozen shredded coconut (can be found at the frozen section at Asian grocery stores). Dry shredded coconut doesn't work well for this recipe. You can use a round pan instead of square

This dessert is amazingly delicious; creamy, sweet, and a little bit tangy. Not to mention, extremely healthy!

Step 1: Gather Ingredients and Tools

Ingredients for one small serving:
- ¼ medium avocado
- 1½ shots of vanilla coconut milk
- about half a lime
- honey (to taste)

Tools:
- preparation bowl
- custard cup (if you want)
- fork
- spoon
- measuring device
- cheese grater

Step 2: Mash it Up!

I don't have a blender . . . luckily for me I like chunky foods. Squeeze 1–2 small slices of lime and mash a quarter of a ripe avocado until it's pretty smooth.

Step 3: Add the Milk, Honey, and Maybe Some More Lime . . .

Add the coconut milk and a generous squeeze of honey. Stir until frothy and give it a taste, adding more lime or honey as needed.

Step 6: Eat Up!

It's ready to enjoy!

Notes: I don't have calorie information for this because it varies a lot depending on the size of your avocado. But the general rule of thumb is 50 calories per ounce of avocado, and vanilla coconut milk has 90 calories per cup. All this to say, avocado is great for you so feel free to indulge in a large helping or two any time of the day!

Also, it's tasty without lime if lime isn't your thing.

Step 4: Chill It!

Stick the bowl in the freezer, stirring every 15 minutes. Total time will vary depending on your serving size and freezer temperature, but the mixture should be an ice cream consistency within 30 to 40 minutes, if not sooner.

Step 5: Zest It!

Grate some lime rind on your avocado cream just before serving (this really "makes" it). Garnish with a small lime slice if you want.

Sweet Potato Pie

by jessyratfink
www.instructables.com/id/
sweet-potato-pie-1/

This homemade sweet potato pie is super easy to throw together and it can be easily scaled up to create an army of pies.

I like to use fresh sweet potatoes instead of canned ones—they give the pie a chunkier texture and they're much less sweet! This way you can also control exactly what goes into the pie.

You can use any crust you like, too—the sweet potato filling goes well with graham cracker crusts and pastry crusts. This time I cheated and went with store bought crusts—though I think this sweet potato pie would be really good with my bacon fat piecrust.

Step 1: Ingredients

- 2 cups mashed sweet potatoes (see below)
- ½ cup sugar
- ½ cup unsweetened coconut milk/soy milk/regular milk
- 2 large eggs, beaten
- 2 tablespoons cornstarch
- 1 teaspoon ground cinnamon
- ½ teaspoon ground ginger
- pinch of cloves
- ½ teaspoon salt
- piecrust of choice

I fully own up to cheating on the crust this time. I was having a busy day and didn't do my prep the night before. I was also making two pies, so I doubled the ingredient list above.

You'll also need to preheat your oven to 325° F.

To prep the sweet potatoes, I find it is easiest to cut them in half, pierce them with a sharp pairing knife in several places, and pop them in the microwave until they're nice and soft. This also retains more of the flavor than boiling them does. Boiling also runs the risk of leaving you with watery mash, which can make a pie that doesn't firm up.

Once they're soft, take the skin off and mash them—don't be too meticulous about mashing, some small chunks are okay and they make the texture of the pie really lovely.

Step 2: Mix in the Dry Stuff

Combine your cornstarch, clove, cinnamon, ginger, and salt in a small bowl. Mix it together with a fork and then pour it over the sweet potato mash.

Now stir it into the mash—keep going until you can't see any dry bits.

Whisk this together for a minute or two, until everything is well combined. If you see any HUGE pieces of sweet potato, feel free to break them up.

Step 3: Add the Wet Ingredients

Add the eggs, milk, and sugar to the bowl. At this point it's best to switch out the potato masher for a big whisk.

Step 4: Pour Into your Crust and Bake!

You'll be baking it at 325° F for 50–60 minutes, depending on how hot your oven runs. Mine is always feeling a little low and slow, so I do an hour.

You'll know they're done once the crust is nicely browned and the middle of the pie is totally firm. Grab the pie with a couple of pot holders and shake it gently side to side. If it wiggles, put it back in for five minutes. If it doesn't, it's done.

Step 5: Cooling and Serving

Cooling your pie is essential to getting nice, clean slices. If you don't care what it looks like, you can start eating immediately after the sweet potatoes stop being food lava.

I waited for about an hour before I dug in, and it was still pretty warm. You can speed up the cooling process by putting the pie pans on a wire rack.

It's really great all by itself or with vanilla bean ice cream or cool whip. And now I need to go eat another piece, I think.

(Pi)ña Colada

by marythomas
www.instructables.com/id/
Pina-Colada-2/

A simple and festive no-bake pie recipe in a cup. A perfect complement to any Pi day celebration!

Step 1: Ingredients

- 2 (6 oz.) cans of pineapple juice
- 1 can coconut milk
- 1½ teaspoons rum extract
- 1 (3.4 oz) box vanilla instant pudding
- 1 cup shredded coconut
- 1 carton heavy whipping cream
- ½ teaspoon vanilla extract
- ¼ cup sugar
- 1 package (12–16) lemon ginger snaps
- several large pineapple spears

Step 2: Combine Liquid

In a large bowl, combine nectar, coconut milk, and 1 teaspoon rum extract. Sprinkle pudding mix over liquid and whisk for 2 minutes.

Step 3: Whip Cream

Using an electric mixer, whisk entire carton of heavy whipping cream, adding in sugar, vanilla extract, and ½ teaspoon rum extract.

Step 4: Fold in Whipped Cream

Fold in half of the whipped cream.

Step 5: Crush Ginger Snaps

Crush ginger snaps between waxed paper using a rolling pin.

Step 6: Fill Goblets

Press crumb crust into bottom of goblet. Pour mixture on top of crust. Fill about half the glass. Chill in refrigerator for 3 hours.

Step 7: Remove Goblet from Refrigerator.

Top with remaining whipped cream and coconut.

Step 8: Cut Pineapple into Pi Symbol.

Use toothpicks to hold pieces together. Place on edge of goblet and serve!

Malaysian Coconut Balls

by Scriptone
www.instructables.com/id/
Onde-Onde-Malaysian-
Coconut-Balls/

Try this soft, scrumptious, and delicious dessert (often served at yumcha) known also as mochi to the Japanese. It's a tweak on the normal green onde onde—when you've run out of pandan leaves.

This recipe is steamed and uses similar ingredients as the deep-fried Jin Dou—a birthday or Chinese New Year snack covered with crunchy sesame seeds.

Gluten-free as well, but I reckon the GI must be pretty high.

Step 1: Ingredients

Ingredients for Onde Onde (Makes 12)

- 220gm glutinous rice flour
- 100gm sugar
- 250ml coconut milk
- cornstarch for rolling

Place flour, sugar, and coconut milk in food processor. Add more water if dry.

Whizz until it appears like the soft, runny cake mixture below.

Place in shallow dish and steam 20–30 minutes until cooked.

NEW UPDATE

You may speed up the cooking process by microwaving the mixture in a deep bowl for 2 minutes on high.

Stir the half cooked mixture thoroughly

Zap again on high for 2–3 more minutes till your dough is opaque.

Cool slightly before filling with fillings.

Roll on chopping board dusted with cornstarch, chop into 12 pieces.

This had great results for me, turned out extremely soft and chewy and didn't turn hard until DAY 3 in the fridge.

Step 2: Red Bean Filling

Ingredients:

- cooked red beans
- ½ cup gula melaka
- palm sugar

Add melted palm sugar to red beans and mash for a chewy, textured filling.

Blend if you prefer a finer texture.

Step 3: Pecan Nut and Coconut Filling

Ingredients:

- ¼ cup chopped pecans
- 3 tablespoons shredded coconut
- ¼ cup melted gula melaka
- palm sugar with 3 tablespoons water

Mix all ingredients together.

Step 4: Knead the Steamed Dough

This step is optional. Place the steamed dough into mixer and knead for 10 minutes with dough attachment.

Step 5: Assemble Coconut Balls

Pan-fry extra the glutinous rice flour for 3 minutes over medium heat. You could use raw cornstarch instead as it is safe to eat.

One site recommends: "Researchers discovered that uncooked cornstarch dissolved in a non-sugary drink, such as milk or sugar-free soda, helped control diabetics'; blood glucose levels overnight." I'd check that out for accuracy.

(Use for coating hands and forming the coconut balls because the mixture is extremely sticky and gluey.)

Coat hands with raw cornstarch (or pan-fried glutinous rice flour) and insert filling.

This is rather sticky process and impossible without flour. Coat with remaining shredded coconut.

For chefs—here is the (CCC) critical control point. Normally you'd be using gloves and I'm still working on checking if the rice flour is cooked thoroughly before rolling out the balls.

Bake in oven at 200 degree celsius for 20 minutes or until puffy. Turn over after 10 minutes to brown the other side.

Once cooled all the pastries will collapse into a hard mass (as air leaves).

Reheat on cast iron/non-stick pan to soften and serve. (No need to add extra oil)

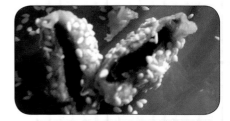

Step 6: Baked Jin Dou— Crunchy Sesame Seed- Coated Ovals (with Savoury Filling)

Savoury filling ingredients:
- 1 cup grated white radish (lopak)
- ½ cup finely chopped cabbage
- ¼ cup red capsicum (peppers)
- ¼ cup finely grated onion

Fry with 2 tablespoons oil until caramelized and fragrant. Cool. You could also fill with sweet red bean mixture if desired.

Fill the prepared steamed glutinous rice flour dough. Flatten dough with dry-fried flour to make it easier to shape.

Mochiko Cake with your Favorite Berries

by c_bluesky
www.instructables.com/id/
Mochiko-Cake-with-your-
favorite-berries/

There was a description of comparison that I learned from a Japanese children's book. When something is delicious, you may say, "It's so yummy in my mouth that my blushing cheeks dropped!"

That is exactly the description I would use for this gluten-free cake. My friends are divided into two groups when tasting it: those who like the gummy chewy center and those who like the savory sweet crust, so I chose to bake it in muffin pans and it turned out perfectly fine to fill two muffin pans.

If you like berries and would want the cake to be more colorful, just drop and distribute one half-pint container of either raspberries, blueberries, or blackberries. One thing I noticed, the berries are better toned when frozen before use.

Step 1: Prepare the Ingredients
Have these at the ready:
- 2 14-oz cans of coconut milk
- 2½ cups cane sugar
- 5 eggs
- 1 box mochiko powder
- 2 teaspoons aluminum-free baking powder
- ¼ teaspoon coarse kosher salt
- 1 teaspoon pure vanilla
- ½ stick butter, melted in the microwave for 45 seconds
- 1 half-pint berries, frozen at least overnight

Step 2: Pick your Weapons
Then prep these:
- Your favorite mixing bowl that doesn't scratch at whisking and is big enough to hold the batter (4-5 quarts' capacity is fine)
- A whisk that is comfortable to use with either hands (you will need the use of both hands—not at the same time together—because one hand only will tire you)
- A teaspoon measuring spoon
- A ramekin to melt the butter in
- Two dozen-size muffin pans
- A can opener for the coconut milk
- A baking spray or a brush to grease the pan (then add butter for greasing)

- A nice smile on your face (it helps to think of good things when baking for people you will share with)
- A small offset spatula
    Preheat oven to 350° F and grease pans with baking spray or softened butter.

Step 3: Whisk, Stir, Switch, Whisk, Stir

Into the mixing bowl, pour:
- One whole can of coconut milk
- All the sugar
- Eggs
    Whisk until sugar is dissolved.

Then, pour in:
- One whole box of mochiko powder
- Salt
- Baking powder
    Stir until you see only a few little lumps. Switch hand if you get tired. Almost there, pour in:
- The second can of coconut milk
- Vanilla
    Whisk gently just to blend. You will see the lumps disappear.

Last, pour in:
- Melted butter
    Stir from edge to center, repeat until uniform color.

Step 4: Get the Cakes in the Oven and Flavor

Pour and distribute batter into the muffin pans. Fill each groove only 5 mm under the rim—just not at all full. Top with your favorite berries—better yet, you may combine two (or three, or four) berries.

By this time, your oven is ready. Bake the cakes for 30 minutes, and then switch (left to right, back to front). Bake 5 more minutes. Take them all out of the oven immediately. Set aside to cool for 15 minutes.

Use a spatula to loosen the edges and scoop cake out. Cool cakes on cookie racks until warm enough to enjoy—no utensils are necessary, little kids will show it to you—just use your hands. The cakes are good at room temperature too, and remember, your friends are still wondering when you'll be bringing in your goodies.

P.S. The other picture shows how they are with frozen blueberries.

Green Tea Mochi Cake

by weekofmenus
www.instructables.com/id/
Green-Tea-Mochi-Cake/

Makes one 9 × 13 pan, or 24 squares.

Green tea and mochi meet together in this wonderful chewy and delicious dessert. The combination of aromatic green tea and unctuous mochi can't be beat. It's simple to make (whisk ingredients together) and the results definitely wow people.

Step 1: Ingredients

- 1 lb box of mochiko flour (3 cups equivalent)
- 2½ cups of sugar
- 2 teaspoons of baking powder
- 4 teaspoons of matcha powder
- ¼ teaspoon salt
- 1 14-oz can of coconut milk—not lowfat
- 1 12-oz can evaporated milk
- 5 large eggs
- 1 stick of butter (½ cup of butter) melted and slightly cooled

Step 2: Method

Preheat oven to 350° F. Grease a 9 × 13 baking pan.

In a large mixing bowl, whisk together mochiko flour, sugar, baking powder, matcha powder, and salt.

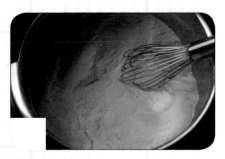

Allow cake to cool for about 30 minutes on a rack, and then carefully flip it out and cut into 24 squares, or the size of your choice. You can store mochi cake for three days, covered.

Step 3: Method

In a separate bowl or large measuring cup (4 cup capacity), beat eggs, and then add coconut milk, evaporated milk, and melted butter.

Carefully pour the wet ingredients over the mochiko flour mixture and whisk until mixture is smooth and uniform in texture.

Pour batter into greased 9 × 13 pan. Carefully smooth out the top.

Step 4: Method

Bake for 90 minutes, until top is golden brown, and the cake begins to pull away from the sides of the pan.

Drinks

Mango Coconut Smoothie

by shy_violet
www.instructables.com/id/
Mango-Coconut-Smoothie/

My ABSOLUTE favorite smoothie EVER! It's tropical but not that ridiculously sweet stereotype of tropical flavors. Natural, cool, and refreshing, it is a gentle vegan reminder of a mango lassi . . .

Ingredients:
- 1 cup fresh or frozen mango
- 3 tablespoons of canned coconut milk
- ¼ to ½ frozen banana slices
- 2 ice cubes

Materials:
- blender or immersion blender
- chilled glass

Directions:
Blend all ingredients together, pour into a chilled glass (if not using an immersion blender), and then consume.

This is an energy boosting drink great for mornings or any time you need a little energy.

Step 1: What You Need
- a blender
- measuring cups
- a couple glasses
- 3 bananas
- 1 cup almond milk or soy milk or milk or any other kind of milk that you might drink
- ground coffee
- sugar
- cocoa
- boiling water
- half a tray of ice
- 1 cup coconut milk

Step 2:
Mix 1 tablespoon of cocoa and 2 tablespoons sugar together and add enough boiling water to make a syrup. Set this aside for later.

Put 2 tablespoons of ground coffee in a mug and fill the mug ¾ of the way with boiling water. Let sit until later.

If you have access to a cafe you can also use 2 or more shots of espresso in this drink instead of the coffee.

Step 3: Mixing Time
Pour the almond milk in the blender, add the chopped up bananas, chocolate syrup you made in the last step, the cup of coffee with grinds of the espresso from the last step, the half tray of ice, and the coconut milk. Blend until smooth, taste test along the way to make sure it taste right for you. Enjoy your "funky monkey" smoothie.

Berry Banana Bash with a Kick

by Kitty Kait
www.instructables.com/id/
Berry-Banana-Bash-with-a-
Kick/

This is a very healthy smoothie that tastes great. An easy great tasting way to get your daily vitamins. No refined sugars added. Makes about 4 smoothies.

- a couple tall glasses
- Ingredients
- 1 cup almond milk (or any other type of milk)
- ⅔ cup coconut milk
- depending on the number of people drinking this batch put in one multi-vitamin per person
- 2 cups berries. If frozen you don't need to add ice, if fresh, add ice
- 2 bananas
- 1 shot lime syrup
- 2 tablespoons ground flax
- 1 shot lemon juice
- ½ cup rolled oats
- ¼ cup guava nectar
- an apple

Step 1: What You Need
- Blender
- measuring cups

Step 2: Mixing Time
Add the milk, coconut milk, vitamins, berries, bananas, lime, flax, lemon, oats, and guava into the blender and blend until smooth. If you are using fresh berries, add half a tray of ice. Enjoy your healthy drink great for breakfasts.

Oven Temperatures

Fahrenheit	Celcius	Gas Mark
225°	110°	¼
250°	120°	½
275°	140°	1
300°	150°	2
325°	160°	3
350°	180°	4
375°	190°	5
400°	200°	6
425°	220°	7
450°	230°	8

Metric and Imperial Conversions
(These conversions have been rounded for convenience)

Ingredient	Cups/Tablespoons/Teaspoons	Ounces	Grams/Milliliters
Butter	1 cup=16 tablespoons=2 sticks	8 ounces	230 grams
Cream cheese	1 tablespoon	0.5 ounce	14.5 grams
Cheese, shredded	1 cup	4 ounces	110 grams
Cornstarch	1 tablespoon	0.3 ounce	8 grams
Flour, all-purpose	1 cup/1 tablespoon	4.5 ounces/0.3 ounce	125 grams/8 grams
Flour, whole wheat	1 cup	4 ounces	120 grams
Fruit, dried	1 cup	4 ounces	120 grams
Fruits or veggies, chopped	1 cup	5 to 7 ounces	145 to 200 grams
Fruits or veggies, pureed	1 cup	8.5 ounces	245 grams
Honey, maple syrup, or corn syrup	1 tablespoon	.75 ounce	20 grams
Liquids: cream, milk, water, or juice	1 cup	8 fluid ounces	240 ml
Oats	1 cup	5.5 ounces	150 grams
Salt	1 teaspoon	0.2 ounces	6 grams
Spices: cinnamon, cloves, ginger, or nutmeg (ground)	1 teaspoon	0.2 ounce	5 ml
Sugar, brown, firmly packed	1 cup	7 ounces	200 grams
Sugar, white	1 cup/1 tablespoon	7 ounces/0.5 ounce	200 grams/12.5 grams
Vanilla extract	1 teaspoon	0.2 ounce	4 grams

also available

Healing Spices
How Turmeric, Cayenne Pepper, and Other Spices Can Improve Your Health, Life, and Well-being

Edited by Instructables.com

Spices not only add a flavorful kick to meals, they also have some amazing benefits to improve certain ailments and improve overall health. Rich in antioxidants and polyphenols, spices and herbs like turmeric, cayenne pepper, cinnamon, ginger, garlic, cloves, coriander, and sage can fight inflammation, protect against chronic conditions, and can even help with losing weight.

Featuring dozens of recipes for meals and beauty remedies, Healing Spices is a great tool for anyone looking to add more flavor to their diet and cut out unhealthy seasonings like salt, sugar, and fatty oils. You'll find great recipes like:

- Chickpea and carrot tangine
- Sweet potato and coconut soup
- Probiotic ginger beer
- Chicken tikka masala with turmeric rice
- Lemon-garlic sorbet
- Cayenne toasts
- Orange, fig, and sage chutney
- Mexican hot chocolate cupcakes
- And much more

There are also remedies for burns, problem skin and hair, losing your voice, toothaches, and a guide detailing the benefits of each spice and herb. Healing Spices is the ultimate compendium for anyone wishing to cook with healthier seasonings.

US $12.95 paperback ISBN: 978-1-62087-697-8

also available

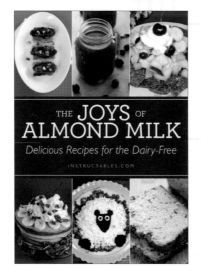

The Joys of Almond Milk
Delicious Recipes for the Dairy-Free
Edited by Instructables.com

Unsweetened almond milk has less than half the calories of skim dairy milk. It has the same consistency of whole milk, and it has more vitamins and minerals than soy milk. If you can handle tree-nuts, then you have no excuse not to use almond milk every day of your life.

With so many diets and eating habits out there—like vegan, gluten-free, and low-carb—it can be confusing to try keeping up with what kind of food is acceptable for specialty eaters. The beauty of almond milk is that it fits all of those eating habits and so many more. Even more perfect is that almond milk can be used in place of dairy, soy, or rice milk in almost any cooking situation.

With these dozens of Instructables recipes in one convenient collection, you'll be on your way to a more almond-based lifestyle in no time! Only in this collection can you find amazing recipes like:

- Raw chocolate almond chia pudding
- Vegan butternut biscuits
- Creamy vegan baked potato soup
- Vegan shepherd's pie
- Healthy chocolate banana bread
- And so much more!

You don't have to be vegan, gluten-free, or even watching your weight to enjoy the healthy benefits of almond milk. With it, you know exactly what you're drinking; with *The Joys of Almond Milk*, you'll know exactly what you're eating, too.

US $14.95 hardcover ISBN: 978-1-62914-800-7

also available

Meatless Eats
Savory Vegetarian Dishes from Around the World
Edited by Sarah James

Originating from Instructables, a popular project-based community made up of all sorts of characters with wacky hobbies and a desire to pass on their wisdom to others, *Meatless Eats* is made up of recipes from a cast of cooks who demonstrate their culinary savvy and flavor combinations.

Meatless Eats gives full step-by-step instructions for creating delicious vegetarian dishes that even die-hard carnivores will crave. Written by cooks who can't get enough of veggies, each recipe contains pictures for an easy follow-along guide, even for those who spend little to no time in the kitchen. Discover your inner vegetarian with these mouthwatering recipes:

- Eggplant Parmesan
- Veggie Mexican Lasagna
- Portobello Mushrooms with Grilled Feta Burger
- Scrumptious Caponata
- Tomato Frittata
- Fiery Pumpkin Samosas
- Vegetarian Mushroom Gravy
And much more!

The Instructables community offers a great mixture of tastes and cuisines. Italian, Mexican, American, and more will appease any picky eater as well as provide for those who are willing to try just about anything. *Meatless Eats* will have you swearing by your healthy lifestyle, even if it's only for a single meal.

US $12.95 paperback ISBN: 978-1-62087-697-8

also available

Amazing Cakes
Recipes for the World's Most Unusual, Creative, and Customizable Cakes

Edited by Sarah James

Rubik's cubes, fire-breathing dragons, jack-o-lanterns, pirate ships, pianos, and Star Wars figurines.

With Instructables.com's *Amazing Cakes*, you'll be able to make cakes shaped like animals, mythical creatures, and vehicles. They may light up, breathe fire, or blow bubbles or smoke. They may be 3D or they may be animated, seeming to move of their own free will. Whether they're cute and cuddly (like a penguin) or sticky and gross (like a human brain!), these cakes have two things in common: They're (mostly) edible and they're amazing! In addition to the cakes mentioned above, you'll also learn how to make cakes shaped like:

- Yoda
- Helicopters
- 3D dinosaurs
- Moving tanks
- Pi signs (p)
- Bass fish

- Zombie heads
- Swimming pools
- Ladybugs
- Evil clowns
- And more!

Instructables.com authors walk you through each step of the process. The photos accompanying the step-by-step directions provide additional information and enable you to compare your final products with the originals.

US $12.95 paperback ISBN: 978-1-62087-697-8